YOUR QUEER CAREER

The Ultimate Career Guide for Lesbian, Gay, Bisexual, and Transgender Job Seekers

RILEY B. FOLDS III, MS*, CDP

Legal Disclaimer

The publisher and the author make no representations or warranties with respect to the accuracy or completeness of the contents of this work and specifically disclaim all warranties, including without limitation warranties of fitness for a particular purpose. No warranty maybe created or extended by sales or promotional materials. The advice and strategies contained herein may not be suitable for every situation.

Neither the publisher nor the author shall be liable for damages arising herefrom. The fact that an organization or website is referred to in this work as a citation and/or a potential source of further information does not mean that the author or the publisher endorses the information the organization or website it may provide or recommendations it may make.

Further, readers should be aware that Internet websites listed in this work may have changed or disappeared between when this work was written and when it is read.

In loving memory of my grandmother,
Frances M. Reid (1924-2013)

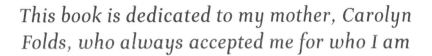

This book is dedicated to my mother, Carolyn Folds, who always accepted me for who I am

and

To all the great LGBTQ workplace advocates who have come before me, those who are currently working tirelessly, and those who will continue to ensure that individuals who identify as LGBTQ can take their whole selves to the workplace without fear.

Acknowledgments

My warmest thanks to all those who have made this book project a reality.

To the thousands of lesbian, gay, bisexual, transgender, and queer college students that I have had the pleasure of meeting and providing perspective on the specific challenges transitioning from academia to the workplace—you all inspire me to keep doing the good work.

To all the bosses that I ever had for never making me feel less of a person and encouraging me to follow my dreams.

To my friends and family who have supported me emotionally throughout the process of coming out and writing this book.

To all the LGBTQ individuals who have ever come out in the workplace—your courage helped pave the way.

Last, but not least, to all the LGBTQ workplace advocates that came before me, thank you for all the ground work. It is because of you that I get to do the work that I love.

Contents

Preface 1

Introduction: LGBTQ at Work 9

Chapter 1.   Reasons for Career Preparation 11

The Challenges You May Face as an LGBTQ Employee 13

Harassment and Discrimination 15

National Laws for LGBTQ Employees 17

State & Local Laws for LGBTQ People in the Workplace 19

ENDA Defined 22

ENDA Timeline 24

4 Exercises in Rights Awareness 27

Chapter 2.   Career Path Self-Assessment 31

Sexual Orientation and Gender Identity
in Career Assessments: Interests 33

Sexual Orientation and Gender Identity
in Career Assessments: Values/Belief System 35

Sexual Orientation and Gender Identity
in Career Assessments: Skills 37

Sexual Orientation and Gender Identity: Barriers 39

Queer Identity Development and Career Identity Development 41

3 Exercises in Career Development 47

Chapter 3. Job Search Factors: Overview............... **49**

Understand What May Happen 52

Know Yourself and Your Career Path 53

Gain Valuable Experience 55

People in the Workplace............................ 56

Getting That Job 58

4 Exercises in Job Search Factors.................... 60

Chapter 4. Finding Successful Role Models & Mentors 63

Who Is a Role Model to You? 65

Bandura's Social Learning Theory 66

What an LGBTQ Role Model Does................... 68

Why You Need an LGBTQ Mentor................... 69

Aligning Your Goals with Your Mentor............... 71

3 Exercises in Finding a Role Model/Mentor 72

Chapter 5. Your LGBTQ-Inclusive Employers **75**

Why LGBTQ-Inclusive Employers? 77

How to Find These Employers...................... 78

The HOT List and the CEI 80

Diversity Inc. Magazine and Company Websites 82

Trade Magazines, Events, Associations 84

5 Exercises in Finding LGBTQ Employers 87

Chapter 6. Creating Your Resume................... **91**

What to Put on Your Resume 93

Should You Be Out and Open?...................... 95

How to Include It in Your Resume 96

Tips on Great Resume Creation 98

The Pros and Cons of LGBTQ Content on Resumes.... 99

Resumes for Those with Limited Professional Experience 101

4 Exercises to Complete a Successful Resume 105

Chapter 7.   Being Successful at Interviews 107

Should You Come Out in the Interview? 109

How to Come Out in an Interview 111

Preparation and Research 113

How to Dress for an Interview 114

Appropriate Behavior at Interviews 117

4 Exercises on Successful Interviewing 120

Chapter 8.   Coming Out at Work 123

When to Come Out at Work 125

How to Come Out at Work 127

Assessing the Office Vibe 128

Why You Should Come Out 130

Weighing the Pros and Cons 132

4 Exercises in Knowing When to Come Out 134

Chapter 9.   Combating Discrimination Based
on Sexual Orientation 137

Defining Discrimination Based on Sexual Orientation
and Gender Identity 139

What to Do if You Face Discrimination 141

Forms of Discrimination 143

Examples of Workplace Discrimination 144

Important Job Rights to Know 146

3 Exercises in Identifying Discrimination 148

Chapter 10. Using Social Media to Find a Job 151

The Use of Social Media by Employers and LGBTQ Job Seekers .. 153

How to Use Search Engine Filters 154

Which Platforms Are Most Useful? 155

Your Mini Social Media Strategy 158

Finding an LGBTQ Friendly Workplace with Social Media 160

4 Exercises in Using Social Media for Job Searches 162

Chapter 11. Career Search Networking 165

How to Network for an Increase in Job Potential 167

LGBTQ Campus Groups and Community Associations 169

How to Form Relationships with Groups and Associations 170

Conferences, Career Fairs, and Recruiting Events 171

Other Networking Opportunities 172

4 Exercises in Career Search Networking 174

Conclusion 177

Useful LGBTQ Resources 181

References 191

About the Author 203

Preface

Writing a book has been a dream of mine since I was a young child. I can recall spending days at a time writing short stories and plays, but as a child would, not thinking much about them afterwards. My mom always thought her son's writings would be published someday. That being said, I do not think either of us thought the book's premise would be a career resource guide for lesbian, gay, bisexual, transgender, and queer (LGBTQ) job seekers. In any case, now was the right time to take on this project.

If you had told me in high school or college that I was going to be a well-respected and recognized advocate for LGBTQ workplace equality, I would have called you crazy. Fast forward to today. If you ask me if there was anything else I would rather be than an LGBTQ workplace equality advocate, I would call you crazy. It is one of many stories that I share with students. The lesson here is that career development is a life-long journey and there are many paths one can go down. Factors such as self-discovery, interests, education, and economic factors, along with personal and professional experiences can change who we are. This can lead us down different professional roads.

I want to clarify a couple of items before moving forward. First, this book is not advocating for everyone to be out and open about their sexual orientation or gender identity in the workplace. Just as coming out personally can be a challenging and difficult decision, so too is the decision to come out in the workplace. Also, like coming out personally, it is a continual process.

Hopefully, the information in this resource guide will lead you to consider where you are personally and professionally in regards to your queer identity and career development. I have spent most of my adult life spanning the spectrum of being closeted in the workplace to full integration of my queer identity into my work-life.

Second, I want to establish the use of the term queer in this book. I use the term as a blanket and inclusive term for the entire community. Years ago, the term queer had a negative association to it. However, members of Generation Y have increasingly reclaimed the term with positivity, pride, and inclusion. Further, often you will see and hear the acronym LGBTQ as an inclusive term. While it is used interchangeably in this book with queer and recognized as a unifying term, the literal acronym cannot represent the entire community. Pansexuals, questioning individuals, intersexed individuals, two-spirits, and many other identities exist and should be recognized. I fully appreciate that our community is made up of many identities; each having their own challenges and needs when addressing career development.

The experience of coming out professionally can be similar to coming out personally. For me, coming out to my friends and family did not take shape until after leaving college. In regards to coming out professionally, it would take years after that for me to finally feel comfortable doing so. Many would consider me a late bloomer. Instead of boring with you the all the juicy details of how I got from a state of identity confusion to one of identity synthesis, I will share a few vignettes of my experiences in the workplace.

The first occurred about four years after I graduated from college. I was working at the National Democratic Institute (NDI) as an International Operations Officer. Personally, I was beginning to explore my sexual orientation in Washington, DC. However, professionally I was 100% in the closet. The work environment at NDI was very young, open, and social. However, I found myself limiting interaction with coworkers out of fear of being discovered. Common questions such as "How was your weekend?" and "Are you dating anyone?" would make me sweat. I would commonly change pronouns to chat about guys that I had interest in and names of gay bars or clubs that I frequented. I will never know who bought the cover stories and who did not. However, as time went on and stronger bonds with coworkers formed, I felt guilty about lying to them. Further, I began dating someone significant. From their perspective, it would appear that my special friend and I were spending a lot of time together, even moving in together!

Over time, I began feeling as if I wanted to look for another organization to work for and decided that, when the opportunity presented itself, I would be out from day one. In the meantime, I decided to come out to one person at NDI. After I told her, I felt as if our relationship suffered. I do not think she judged me for being gay, but I sensed a feeling of how could I keep something like this from her for so long. A level of trust seemed violated. We both left the company soon after and lost touch personally and professionally. I always felt sadness over it.

My next position was at Chemonics International. Like NDI, Chemonics was filled with twenty-something do-gooders who wanted to change the world. I say that in a positive way. I was one of them. Also like NDI, it was considered a very open-minded organization. I had made the decision that I was going to be out from day one. I formed the mantra, "I'm here, queer, and deal with it!" I had learned from my closeted NDI experience.

The first day on the job at Chemonics my direct supervisor, Bill, proudly walked me around the office and introduced me to what seemed to be everyone in the building. Casually walking back to our cubicles he said, "I am sure that I will get plenty of phone calls about you this afternoon from interested girls that we saw today." I was flattered for a moment. Then I started to have a dialog in my head that seemed to last much longer than the seconds it actually did. Did he just say girls? Isn't this the open door I have been waiting for? I told myself, "March through it with a rainbow flag in hand." But all the fears of not being accepted and of being isolated, professionally and socially, came rushing over me. The feeling swept me and my flag right back into the closet. I felt sick and walked into my cubical defeated. That afternoon I should have been reviewing all the systems and files to make my new job easier. Although it may have appeared that I was doing just that, I was weighed down with a sense that I just failed Chemonics, Bill, the community I was starting to feel a part of, and myself. How could I be such a coward?

That night I discussed it with my partner at the time, Nikko, and made the decision to correct my wrong. I could barely sleep that night. The next morning I was at the office before anyone else. I sat there, poised, ready. Again it was hard to concentrate on much else. The clock struck nine, and Bill came zipping past my cubicle to get to his. Before he had his coat off and messenger bag on the floor, I appeared sitting in the guest chair across from his desk. I confronted him about the comment he made the day before about the girls calling about me. I told him that I was flattered, but that I was in a relationship...with a guy. There was a pause, brief I am sure, but it seemed to last minutes. Then Bill said, "Oh, you do not even seem gay." I think I sighed in relief and laughed, but again, in my head thought, "What did that mean?" Later, I asked myself, "Was Bill only exposed to the gay parade stereotype to which he was contrasting me with?" Would my sexual orientation not be such an issue, since I obviously could fly under the radar and appear straight?

Those questions would be answered in time. The battle of the day was won, and I could focus on learning all about my new position and the company. Oh, and one thing you can always rely on is the office gossip mill. I am sure by the end of that working day many were aware that I was playing for the boys' team.

My time at Chemonics was beneficial professionally and emotionally. Unlike my years at NDI, it was refreshing to talk about what Nikko and I did over the weekend or where we wanted to go on vacation. We spend more time at work than we do awake with our partners, family members, friends, and pets. Our coworkers become our families. The workplace is a blend of professional and personal aspects that converge five days a week. I can recall the fun Nikko I had together at the company holiday party. Introducing him as my partner, not friend or roommate, was empowering and comforting. I felt a bond with my colleagues at Chemonics that I wish I had had at NDI.

Another contrast between NDI and Chemonics had to do with the issue of adding Nikko as a domestic partner on my health insurance plan. At NDI, I went to Mary in the human resources department to inquire about doing so. Behind closed doors, I basically came out to her by explaining that I wanted to add Nikko to my health insurance. She was the only other person at NDI that I ever told. She seemed nervous, but provided me the information and forms needed. I always had the feeling Mary's lips were loose and that she had mentioned my request to others. In any case, she failed to mention that NDI did not gross up the tax portion of the benefit the company paid for the domestic partner. However, the organization did absorb the cost for an opposite sex spouse. So my first paycheck after making the request was dinged harshly. Not only was I paying a higher premium, I was paying an outrageous amount in addition for being gay and adding Nikko. I marched back into Mary's office and said thanks, but no thanks. Ever hear that phrase equal but different? Well, there you had it. At Chemonics, it was the polar opposite experience. In my benefits package, I elected to add my partner and paid the premium that any heterosexual couple would. No fuss, no muss!

My last story involves the dilemma discussed in this book and that I have spoken about many times at conferences and workshops: whether or not to be out on a resume or interview. I was submitting my resume for a diversity consultant position at Pepco, the electric utility in Washington, DC. From doing my research, I had an understanding that the corporate culture was conservative. By then I had acquired LGBTQ workplace-specific professional experience. I founded and operated the only nonprofit organization that focused on educating, preparing, and empowering LGBTQ college students for the transition from academia to the workplace. In addition, I had spoken at national conferences and produced reference materials. However, when crafting my resume, I decided to consciously use acronyms and the word diversity instead of spelling out lesbian, gay, bisexual, transgender, and queer.

The choice yielded an interview. I was fully aware that I would be asked about my professional experiences. As I walked into the interview, I made the decision that I would speak openly about working within the queer community. I had taken show and tell materials that exemplified my successes. I left feeling good about myself. If I got the job, it would be great, I thought. If I didn't, at least I felt that I had crossed into full integration as it related to my gay identity and career development.

I got the job and later learned that the diversity department was interested in creating a corporate-wide training on the subject of LGBTQ-inclusiveness in the workplace. I conclude that if I had hidden who I was via the work that I did, I would have never got the job. Further, there was no big coming out moment for me at Pepco. It was just a part of me. I was able to talk about my personal relationships while eating lunch with others, discuss honestly what I did over the weekend, and even hang a sign for queer equality in my cubical without fear of being excluded or harassed.

In closing, what I want to exemplify here is that there is no checklist or right way to be a queer employee. There is only the path that is right for you. This book provides information. Take the approach that it is a salad bar, and you can pick and choose what you want. You do not have to agree with everything in this resource. Also, remember you can always come back for seconds—meaning that, as you progress trying to understand your own intersection of queer identity and career development, you can refer to this book as a continued resource. I hope that this book will help you achieve all the success that you desire. Be true to yourself, and you will not go wrong.

LGBTQ at Work

There are millions of lesbian, gay, bisexual, transgender, and queer (LGBTQ) job seekers struggling to find careers and even hold down a job due in part because of their sexual orientation and gender identity.

While the workplace is progressing, inclusiveness for the LGBTQ community still needs to be advocated. A lot can be unfair with the way queer employees can be treated in the workplace. Just as women and other minorities have unjustifiably faced and continue to face discrimination in the workplace, queer individuals lack the protection of a federal law to curb against such actions. This should be considered the next chapter of civil rights.

From an international perspective, America is sorely behind on gay rights in the workplace. According to a recent report[1] from the International Lesbian, Gay, Bisexual, Trans and Intersex Association (IGLA), Israel, Mozambique, Greece, Norway, and Ireland are just a few of the countries that prohibit employment discrimination based on sexual orientation. The same report highlights that Australia, Sweden, Croatia, and Germany prohibit employment discrimination based on gender identity. Until the U.S. steps up for comprehensive employment nondiscrimination, LGBTQ job seekers should be equipped with the tools and knowledge needed to make a great career in this occasionally hostile environment.

The truth is that being a job seeker and a member of the

---

1   ILGA State-Sponsored Homophobia Report and Gay and Lesbian rights maps, http://ilga.org/ilga/en/article/1161

LGBTQ community can be difficult. Your sexual orientation and gender identity may matter to some people. If you choose to be a teacher—will parents want a homosexual instructing their kids? If hostility presents itself, how will this affect you professionally and personally? You may have more to think about than you know. If you become a lawyer, will you be afforded the same respect as other lawyers in the firm? The answer may be no. There are numerous cases annually of queer job seekers being discriminated against in the workplace.

Lesbians, gays, bisexuals, and transgender individuals are fired every day because of who they are and not for the work they have done. This is the biggest and most dangerous form of discrimination. That is why you need to find the career that will best suit your interests and allow you to be the person you want to be. When you are equipped with the right knowledge, processes, and plans—the world can be yours. It can be hard out there, and you may need a way to defend yourself. As an LGBTQ job seeker, you can still reach the very top of your field. However, in the current climate, it may take some extra work, planning, and strategy to get there.

If you soak up the knowledge and expertise that this book has to offer, you can better prepare yourself for situations that could occur as you journey down your career path. It is a good idea to learn how to protect and defend yourself against discrimination and how to lead yourself down the right path so that you can experience success in your career. After all, careers do help define us as individuals, which is why this book is the beginning of your new life as a career-driven LGBTQ person.

CHAPTER 1

Reasons for Career Preparation

Nothing happens in the 'real' world unless it first happens in the images in our heads."

GLORIA ANZALDUA
(LESBIAN, AUTHOR)

For LGBTQ individuals, career preparation can easily be THE most important step in your overall career development. This is because it is an opportunity to be informed about the workplace, the difficulties you may encounter, and the laws or policies that could protect you from discrimination.

Heading into a new work situation armed with tools, resources, and information when you are an LGBTQ job seeker can make a positive difference. Heading into a new work situation blind when you are an LGBTQ job seeker is not a good idea. Areas to think about include your own queer identity and career development, the industry and organizations in which you are seeking work, and the state in which you reside. You do not want to end up passing on a great opportunity simply because of non-acceptance of your sexual orientation or gender identity at any level. It is better to be smart, cautious, and prepared.

The Challenges You May Face as an LGBTQ Employee

The real reason that you need to prepare for your career is because there may be a host of challenges that you may face in the workplace. As a queer person, you could come up against questions to answer and situations to defend based on your sexual orientation and gender identity. How you respond can affect you not only professionally, but also personally.

Identifying as a member of the LGBTQ community, you are a considered at times part of an invisible minority. Even though an overwhelming majority of Americans disapprove of discrimination based on sexual orientation and gender identity, there are still few laws that protect you.

⌨ TIP

If you are ever discriminated against, it is important to contact an association such as the American Civil Liberties Union or Lambda Legal. Laws that protect LGBTQ individuals will not be created if injustices are kept silent.

You may have to deal with very real issues such as:

- ▲ How do I find LGBTQ-inclusive employers?
- ▲ Should I be out on my resume?
- ▲ Should I be out at the interview?
- ▲ When is it okay to come out at work?
- ▲ How do I come out at work?
- ▲ When should I keep my sexual orientation/gender identity private?
- ▲ How do I handle discrimination in the workplace?
- ▲ Do I have any legal rights to protect me?

These are just a few of the many questions that you may ask yourself as a queer job seeker. Unlike heterosexual people—who do not need to consider the impact that their sexual orientation and gender identity may have on their career—

you should plan accordingly. For example, avoiding problem areas or having the foresight to commit to a job in an LGBTQ-friendly state or company may save you a lot of personal and professional trauma down the road. In addition, knowing the challenges that you may face will help you prepare mentally for them so that you understand the right course of action to take.

Harassment and Discrimination

Two common challenges that you may face in your career are harassment and discrimination. Let us take a look at these two terms.

Harassment involves systematic or continued actions that are unwanted by the person being impacted. In many cases, queer employees are subject to harassment even though it is not directed at them on a personal level. An example is the homophobic sentiment that goes around the office or homophobic slurs that shed a bad light on queer people. If you hear such comments, it should be considered and dealt with no differently than other comments made about women, people of color, or the physically or mentally challenged.

Discrimination often involves treating a certain group of people differently due to a distinction between members of a majority group and minority group. For LGBTQ individuals, this distinction can involve an individual's sexual orientation and gender identity. Just being suspected of being queer can trigger discrimination that can lead to various outcomes, including being fired.

Employers may not fire you; instead they may hold you back in your career. This can take the form of not including you in meetings or not assigning you to meaningful projects. Further they might promote coworkers with less qualifications or experience in an attempt to have you consider quitting.

Being sidelined or overlooked is still discrimination when it is solely based on the fact that you identify as queer.

There are many other forms of discrimination, such as name-calling, threats of violence, open hatred or homophobia, and actual physical violence against members of the LGBTQ community. According to a report published in the Loyola Law Review[2], LGBT people and their heterosexual coworkers consistently reported having experienced or witnessed discrimination based on sexual orientation or gender identity in the workplace. Further, 37% of lesbian and gay individuals have experienced workplace harassment in the last five years, and 12% had lost a job because of their sexual orientation. The statistics are even worse for those who identify as transgender. The report indicates that 90% of transgender individuals have experienced harassment or mistreatment at work. Further, 47% reported having been discriminated against in hiring, promotion, or job retention because of their gender identity.

It is an unfortunate reality that, as an LGBTQ person, you may be harassed and discriminated against more than once in your career. Whether it is a colleague or a supervisor that discriminates against you—it is up to YOU to do something about it. You can limit or prevent harassment and discrimination by making good choices about where you work and whom you work for. Also, you can make sure that if something terrible occurs at work, you know your rights.

The workplace has a long way to go until it is as inclusive of queer employees as it should be. There is nothing inclusive about allowing private companies to terminate the

---

2   Jennifer C. Pizer, Brad Sears, Christy Mallory, and Nan D. Hunter, *Evidence of Persistent and Pervasive Workplace Discrimination Against LGBT People: The Need for Federal Legislation Prohibiting Discrimination and Providing for Equal Employment Benefits*, 45 Loy. L.A. L. Rev. 715 (2012). http://digitalcommons.lmu.edu/llr/vol45/iss3/

employment of people because the powers to be hold biases against individuals who openly identify as or are perceived to be lesbian, gay, bisexual, transgender, or queer.

The first step to becoming an informed LGBTQ person focused on career development is to know your rights. Right now there are employees in the closet because they are afraid that they may be judged and dismissed from their job based on something so private and inconsequential to work. If you are going to limit the harassment and discrimination that individuals in the workplace may throw at you, then you might need some help. You are also going to need a crash course in federal, state, and local rights.

National Laws for LGBTQ Employees

The United States Congress has not yet passed a federal law that fully protects you should a coworker or employer wrongfully harass or discriminate against you. Being persecuted because of your sexual orientation or gender identity is something that should not happen in the workplace—yet it does daily, all across the country.

In lieu of such action by Congress, Presidents Clinton and Obama have advocated for LGBTQ workplace equity in the federal government and agencies. One example includes Executive Order 13087, which reinforces the commitment to non-discrimination in the federal workforce with explicit protections based on sexual orientation. Another is the Memorandum on Federal Benefits and Non-Discrimination[3], which provides guidance prohibiting discrimination based on gender identity.

---

3   Memorandum For The Heads Of Executive Departments And Agencies. The White House: Press Release. http://www.whitehouse.gov/the_press_office/Memorandum-for-the-Heads-of-Executive-Departments-and-Agencies-on-Federal-Benefits-and-Non-Discrimination-6-17-09

In a landmark ruling in 2012, the U.S. Equal Employment Opportunity Commission (EEOC) determined that job bias against employees on the basis of gender identity amounts to sex discrimination under existing law. The EEOC is the federal agency that interprets and enforces federal non-discrimination laws. Title VII of the Civil Rights Act of 1964 prohibits employment discrimination based on race, color, religion, sex, and national origin. It should be noted that the ruling is binding only to agencies under the EEOC's jurisdiction.

In every other sector, employers can choose to base their decisions on biased, discriminatory sentiments. They can fire you —even if you have worked with them for years—if they discover or suspect that you are queer. Chances are that the organization will not come out and say they fired you because of your sexual orientation or gender identity. Usually it is masked as downsizing or low productivity. However, in many states an employer could look you straight in the face and simply say you are being fired for being LGBTQ and you would have no recourse. They could also decide to exclude you from business gatherings, meetings, and perks because you are queer. If you work at a company that has no policy against this kind of action, then you might have to prepare yourself in case you are taken advantage of or treated differently.

There have been many attempts to pass federal legislation that would finally give LGBTQ workers legal rights in the private business sector, but to no avail. Some 61% of all Americans[4] want to see job discrimination based on sexual orientation prohibited at a federal level. Every year more support grows for the federal act. But the law has not yet been

---

4   Issue: Federal Advocacy, Employment Non-Discrimination Act, http://www.hrc.org/laws-and-legislation/federal-legislation/employment-non-discrimination-act

ratified. In the meantime, while LGBTQ associations and pro-equality politicians fight to get this legislation noticed, you will have to find a way to have a successful career.

If you are worried about national law, or the lack of, then you can add your voice to the struggle and sign petitions or become active in an LGBTQ association. Right now the only law advancing is the Employment Non-Discrimination Act (ENDA). This law will go into place once Congress actually ratifies the bill. Then, you can worry a little less about being fired because you are queer. With our voices speaking out, homophobic discrimination in federal law will not last forever!

State & Local Laws for LGBTQ People in the Workplace

Where Congress has failed to act, state governments have stepped in to provide employment protections to the LGBTQ workforce. Wisconsin was the very first state to enact anti-discrimination[5] laws for LGBTQ employees back in 1982. Shortly after that, many other states followed suit. Currently 21 states and the District of Columbia (DC) have passed laws prohibiting employment discrimination based on sexual orientation. Sixteen states and DC also prohibit discrimination based on gender identity[6].

⅄ **States that prohibit discrimination based on sexual orientation and gender identity:** *California, Colorado, Connecticut, District of Columbia, Illinois, Iowa, Massa-*

---

5   Issue: Federal Advocacy, Employment Non-Discrimination Act, http://www.hrc.org/laws-and-legislation/federal-legislation/employment-non-discrimination-act

6   Corporate Equality Index 2013. *Rating American Workplaces on Lesbian, Gay, Bisexual and Transgender Equality.* http://www.hrc.org/files/assets/resources/CorporateEqualityIndex_2013.pdf

chusetts, Maine, Minnesota, New Jersey, New Mexico, Nevada, Oregon, Rhode Island, Vermont, and Washington

⅄ **States that prohibit discrimination based on sexual orientation:** *In addition to the states above -- Delaware, Maryland, New Hampshire, New York, and Wisconsin*

LGBTQ people often choose to live in areas where there are anti-discrimination laws because it makes a difference to their careers. Nearly 50% of all LGBTQ people[7] consciously choose to move to or stay in a liberal and gay-friendly state.

Keep in mind that there are different laws for sexual orientation discrimination and gender identity discrimination. States define the two terms differently, and they fall under separate laws. To clarify, sexual orientation refers to an individual's attraction to another—emotionally, romantically, and/or sexually. Gender identity refers to an individual's sense of oneself as male, female, or gender fluid. If an individual's gender identity and biological sex are not congruent, the individual may identify as transsexual or transgender. Gender identity should not be confused with the term gender expression. Gender expression refers to the way in which a person acts to communicate gender. Examples may include: type of clothing, communication patterns, and interests. Your gender expression may or may not be consistent with socially prescribed gender roles and may or may not reflect one's gender identity.

From a job seeker perspective, interest in becoming a hair stylist or nurse may be stereotyped as effeminate and acceptable roles for women, while a pilot or law enforcement officer is deemed butch and labeled as men's work. Clashing with these stereotypes could result in harassment in the workplace.

7　IREM Legislative Staff, Laws Prohibiting Discrimination Based on Sexual Orientation and Gender Identity, July 2007, http://www.irem.org/pdfs/publicpolicy/Anti-discrimination.pdf

🔍 FACT

The Southeast and Midwest states are the most non-responsive to laws that give LGBTQ employees rights in the workplace, whereas the Northeast and Southwest are the most accommodating. Georgia, Florida, Alabama, and Texas do not recognize your rights, while New Jersey, Washington, Oregon, and California do.

There are various types of coverage that the law provides in different states. For example, Minnesota prohibits gender identity discrimination and sexual orientation discrimination, but Wisconsin has no laws yet on gender identity—they only cover sexual orientation. In this way, certain states offer better protection for the LGBTQ community.

California, for example, prohibits sexual discrimination based on sexual orientation in housing, private and public employment, and public accommodation. They also have sound gender identity laws, and employees are permitted to dress consistently with their chosen gender identity.

It is recommended that you ALWAYS check on your state or local laws to see if you have legal protections when you take on a job in the private sector. Nevada, for example, protects LGBTQ employees, but Arizona does not. If there is no STATE law governing employment, then check to see if the selected organization has non-discrimination policies in place. You should also research loopholes in the policy or law. For example, a company with fewer than 15 people may not have to abide by anti-discrimination laws. Exemptions for religious organizations and religiously affiliated entities exist as well.

> ## 🔍 FACT
>
> There are more than Seven million LGBTQ people in the US; of that amount, 48%[8] choose to remain secretive about their sexuality in the workplace. Recent stats indicate that denying LGBTQ people equal access to family benefits and workplace opportunities is resulting in poverty in many gay and lesbian communities.

ENDA Defined

The Employment Non-Discrimination Act (ENDA) essentially prohibits discrimination based on both gender identity and sexual orientation. It is the leading piece of legislature that has been drafted to uphold the rights of LGBTQ people in the workplace. [8]

While ENDA has not yet been ratified, attempts to get this law passed are being made on a continuous basis. The act was modeled on the Civil Rights Acts of 1964, which also prevents any sort of discrimination based on race, religion, or gender. If this act becomes law, then it can protect millions of LGBTQ employees from experiencing psychological trauma from discrimination during their careers. The great thing about ENDA is that it is a base act. That means that it does not afford LGBTQ people any special rights; it simply extends basic rights to a minority group that is being treated unfairly on a daily basis.

---

8   48% of Gays Aren't Out at Work, Even on Diversity Day, http://www.autostraddle. com/48-of-gays-and-lesbians-still-arent-out-at-work-95205/

ENDA does make what the employer can and cannot do very clear. It does not encourage preferential treatment, but it strongly prohibits discrimination. The workplace is leaning towards accepting ENDA[9]. According to *Fortune Magazine*, 88% of *Fortune 500*[10] companies in the U.S. already have non-discrimination policies in play based on sexual orientation. In contrast, only 57% of the same *Fortune 500* companies have non-discrimination policies based on gender identity. Further, 62% provide domestic partner health benefits, and 25% provide trans-inclusive benefits. This means that companies are warming up to the idea that ENDA could be good for everyone. In fact, the Business Coalition for Workplace Fairness is a group of leading U.S. employers that support ENDA. Bank of America Corp., Best Buy, Chevron, Coca-Cola, Electronic Arts Inc., General Mills, Google, and Microsoft are just a few of the businesses affiliated with the coalition.

Even though laws are created and enforced to the best of the state's ability, discrimination will not disappear completely because it is based on personal sentiment. Women, for example, still struggle to be promoted above men in the workplace, and minorities often report that they have to work twice as hard at times to reach top positions in an organization.

---

9   The Recent ENDA Hearing and What It Means to the LGBT Community, http://outandequal.wordpress.com/2012/06/14/the-recent-enda-hearing-what-it-means-to-the-lgbt-community/

10 LGBT Equality at The Fortune 500, http://www.hrc.org/resources/entry/lgbt-equality-at-the-fortune-500

ENDA Timeline

1994	Employment Non-Discrimination Act first introduced
	Senate Labor and Human Resources Committee holds first hearings on ENDA
1995	ENDA of 1995 introduced
1996	First hearings held on ENDA in the House in Government Programs Subcommittee of the Committee on Small Business
	First floor vote held on ENDA
	Senate rejects it
1997	ENDA of 1997 introduced
	Hearings held by Senate Labor and Human Resources Committee
1998	President Clinton issues Executive Order 13087 prohibiting discrimination based on sexual orientation in much of the federal civilian workforce
	House of Representatives rejects Hefley Amendment to FY 1999 Commerce, Justice, State appropriations bill, which sought to prohibit use of federal funds to enforce the executive order

1999	ENDA of 1999 introduced
2001	ENDA of 2001 introduced
2002	Hearings on ENDA held before Senate Health, Education, Labor and Pensions Committee; Committee favorably reported the bill, which was placed on Senate Calendar
2003	ENDA of 2003 introduced
2007	ENDA of 2007 introduced in April, for the first time inclusive of gender identity

Hearing held by Health, Employment, Labor and Pensions Subcommittee of House Committee on Education and Labor. Sexual orientation-only version of ENDA introduced

Markup held by House Education and Labor Committee; first House floor vote on a version of ENDA

House passes sexual orientation-only bill |

ENDA Timeline (Contd)

2009	ENDA of 2009 introduced in June
	The House Education and Labor Committee held a full committee hearing on the bill in September
	Senate Committee on Health, Education, Labor and Pensions (HELP) held a hearing on ENDA in November
2010	ENDA of 2010 introduced in March
	Congress closes without voting on ENDA, requiring the bill to be reintroduced at a future date
	The 60 votes needed in the Senate to overcome a filibuster could not be obtained
2011	ENDA of 2011 introduced in April but not enacted
2012	Senate Committee on Health, Education, Labor and Pensions (HELP) held a hearing on ENDA in June
2013 (At the time of publication)	ENDA introduced in April to the Senate by Sens. Jeff Merkley (D-OR), Tom Harkin (D-IA), openly gay Sen. Tammy Baldwin (D-WI), and Republican Sens. Mark Kirk of Illinois, and Susan Collins of Maine

4 Exercises in Rights Awareness

1. *Recall and shade in the states on the map below which have passed laws prohibiting employment discrimination based on sexual orientation, gender identity, and both.*

A: See list on pages 19 & 20

2. *What is the difference between law and organizational policy?*

A: Laws must be followed by citizens, public figures, and companies, while policies need only be adhered to by people within the private organization. Laws are created by legislatures and are enforceable by the judicial system.

3. *Jennifer took a job as a sales rep for a food and beverage company and was making excellent progress in her career, selling more product than anyone else on her team for three months consecutively. Jennifer was invited to a work function, where she revealed that her partner was a woman. In the weeks that followed, Jennifer noticed that her team and bosses distanced themselves from her. Then she was fired, due to the company downsizing, though someone else replaced her shortly after that.*

a. How would you have reacted to this situation?

b. Should Jennifer have contested the dismissal?

c. What could Jennifer have done differently to improve this situation?

d. Which state laws or organizational policies would protect you in this instance?

4. What would ENDA mean to you, as a queer person?

A: It would give you rights to not be discriminated against in the workplace based on your sexual orientation or gender identity.

CHAPTER 2

Career Path
Self-Assessment

Success is knowing who you are. If you don't like yourself, change."

RAMON CORTINES
(GAY, EDUCATOR)

Generally speaking, LGBTQ people may bloom later in their careers than heterosexual people. This is thought to be due in part because while growing up, most individuals begin to explore their sexual orientation, gender identity, and vocational interests at about the same time. Queer people may focus on coming to terms with their sexual and gender identity, and have less time to focus on career development. That means that many LGBTQ people feel a little behind when it comes to planning and executing a career. Suddenly you realize that work is important, and that it needs to be as much a part of you as your sexual identity and gender identity. But how do you make this happen? Perform a career development self-assessment of course!

Sexual Orientation and Gender Identity in Career Assessments: Interests

Your career-based interests are an important factor that you need to explore before you begin to plan your career. Self-assessment is really the foundation for finding an appropriate career that you will enjoy.

A key motivating factor for all work is how INTERESTED you are in it. With that consideration, it makes sense to say that exploring a vocation that you are incredibly interested in is the best thing to do. Generally, individuals tend to succeed when something holds their interest and drives them forward.

👤💭 SOMETHING TO THINK ABOUT

Worry about sexual orientation/gender identity by LGBTQ people may cause disruptions early on in life, which causes delays in career development. Because 'self-efficacy' (one's confidence in his or her ability to perform a task) may be lacking in LGBTQ people. It is something you may need to work on to progress in your career.

When you are interested in the work you do, you will most likely develop your skills faster and become better at your job because you are curious and inspired by it. It is suggested that 60% of job satisfaction[11] is finding an area that interests you.

It may be helpful if you list your interests so that you can see and evaluate them. Include everything that interests you— leisure activities, volunteer work, hobbies, and coursework. Now think about the impact your sexual orientation and gender identity has had on the formation of your interests. Consider the following:

- ⚠ Are the books you read LGBTQ-themed in nature?
- ⚠ Are you attracted to careers that serve the LGBTQ population specifically?
- ⚠ The groups or organizations you belong to are associated with the LGBTQ community?
- ⚠ Is it important that you work with other queer people?
- ⚠ Will your career involve an advocacy role for the queer

---

11 Elaine Pofeldt, "Can't Stand Your Job? Feel Better About It!"
http://money.cnn.com/2012/05/29/pf/job-satisfaction.moneymag/index.htm

community?

Did you respond yes to a majority of the questions? The results should allow you to recognize how sexual orientation and gender identity can influence your interests. Keep these answers in mind throughout your job search.

Sexual Orientation and Gender Identity in Career Assessments: Values/Belief System

Values are the things that you believe are important in the way you live and work. When your actions align with your values life is usually good. However, when actions and values are not in sync you are more likely to be unhappy. Compassion, diversity, teamwork, self-reliance, belonging, and having fun are examples of values. Specific values are not exclusive to heterosexuals or those who identify as LGBTQ. Nevertheless values can be shaped or impacted by one's sexual orientation and gender identity. For example, it is possible that the value of equality for someone who is LGBTQ is of great importance because of their exposure to inequality in their personal and/or professional lives. Think about your top values and how they may have been influenced by your sexual orientation or gender identity.

Considering your values, the workplace, and sexual orientation/gender identity it might mean the world to you that coworkers accept you for who you are—a queer individual. If this is something you need, then aligning these factors can make your personal and professional life more harmonious. When your values match your work environment, you have the room you need to thrive in your career. That being identified, if you pick a work environment that opposes or is in conflict with your values—then you may be miserable in that job.

Think about the value of camaraderie with other coworkers. If this mutual trust and friendship does not exist due to either the disclosure of your sexual orientation/gender identity or the nondisclosure of such information to coworkers and managers you may feel alienated. This could prompt you to leave the job. If you choose not to leave, you could stunt your own full potential by staying with the organization. That is why identifying your core values is a critical part of making the right career choice. Knowing what you want/need and then making sure you get it gives you the tools you need to grow, develop, and climb the ladder in your career.

FACT

Values are what help people develop their identities and ethics as they grow up. Members of the queer community may find their values are different because of the personal experiences they have had. This can influence career choices significantly!

It cannot be stressed enough that values can make the difference in a work environment. If, for example, you know that you need job security, stability, and responsibility—actively seek that out. Further, you may highly value a company with a non-discrimination policy and benefits that are inclusive of LGBTQ individuals. Joining a company that is likely to discriminate against you, hold you back, or make you feel miserable because of your sexual orientation and gender identity may not be acceptable.

Other common examples of values include work/life balance, independence, high salary, recognition, spotlight, enjoying leisure time, pleasure, leadership, adventure, achievement, prestige, and inner harmony. You will need to decide which core values are the most important to you. A lesbian mom may value family and work/life balance over a high salary and prestige. Therefore, she may prefer to find a job where her coworkers and employer share and/or encourage such values.

Sexual Orientation and Gender Identity in Career Assessments: Skills

A skill is a proficiency that is gained through training or experience. Skills are an important component that employers look for in the hiring process. Do you know what your skills are?

You may be surprised at how many skills you have accumulated in your life. Some you may take for granted such as writing and reading. Others may include the ability to speak well in public or find solutions to complex problems using your creativity and past experiences. Individuals sometimes make the mistake of allowing their skill set dictate what they do in their careers. Even if you are only a fairly good salesperson, if that is what interests you most, you can always acquire the skills to become great overtime. Skills are essential to succeed in any career, but they can be learned through further training or on the job. Think about the skills you have and those you may want to gain.

Your skills alone should not dictate your career path, but they should act in coordination with your interests, values, and beliefs. And remember—just because you are really good at something, does not mean that you will enjoy doing

> ## ⌕ FACT
>
> The external environment and wider societal and contextual factors can affect the career development of those in the LGBTQ community. According to some pertinent resources[12], queer people are more inclined to choose creative careers that focus on social interaction.

it every day.

Your sexual orientation and gender identity may impact determining where your skills lie. For example, in your role as an officer in the queer campus/community group you may have gained experience organizing meetings, preparing agendas and taking notes. In addition, you may have also found yourself working in a team environment with a diverse mix of people. Further, you may have developed enhanced public speaking and problem solving skills. All these skills are attractive to potential employers. Aligning your skill set with possible vocational opportunities is key. [12]

There are different types of skills that you can list and harness for your career. There are knowledge-based skills that focus on academic learning or on the job training. Then there are transferable skills that can be used in multiple areas such as time management, using technology, and creativity.

What skills do you consider your strengths? It is common that our most highly prized skill is the one we love the most, which is why we became so good at it in the first place. You will

---

12   Richard Florida, "The Rise of The Creative Class,"
      http://www.washingtonmonthly.com/features/2001/0205.florida.html

need to apply all your skills to your internship or job search. When skills, interests, and values align; you will begin to see the light at the end of the tunnel. With this enlightenment, it will be easier to find a career that complements who you are as an LGBTQ person. Allow your career to be based on these factors, and you will do well.

Example:

- ⅄ Interests include mathematics, science, computers, and health.
- ⅄ Values include a challenging social environment, achievement, innovation, leadership, and respect.
- ⅄ Skills include high aptitude for medical sciences, steady hands, analytical mind, fast learner, and good with data entry.

Add these up and you could become a doctor, surgeon, medical technician, nurse—any one of these may suit you.

Sexual Orientation and Gender Identity: Barriers

As a queer person, you may experience barriers that attempt to prevent you from progressing or entering a certain career choice. Homophobia, perceived inappropriate job choices, social stigmas, stereotypes, and job discrimination are examples of potential barriers. That is why you need to understand what these barriers are and how to deal with them.

- ⅄ **Homophobia:** Homophobia is defined as a range of negative attitudes or feelings towards homosexuality. Anyone in your life can be homophobic at any time.

This can be a very real problem for someone who needs to progress through levels during a career. What if your boss is homophobic? What if members of your team are? It is suggested that you address these issues head-on.

▲ **Perceived Inappropriate Job Choices:** Because being LGBTQ is a statement about your personal sexual identity and gender identity, some people may see you as perverted or a sexual deviant. This makes entering certain careers extremely hard, especially if there are children involved. Camp coordinator, teacher, pediatrician, scout leader—some of the general public still cling to malicious stereotypes and believe these are inappropriate job choices for queer people.

▲ **Social Stigmas:** A social stigma, such as homophobia, is the extreme disapproval of a person based on characteristics that separate them from mainstream members of society. Social stigmas tend to be extremely harmful. Examples include the stigma that being LGBTQ is immoral or that all individuals who identify as queer have HIV.

▲ **Stereotypes:** A stereotype can be described as a widely held, fixed image or idea of a particular person or thing. Encountering LGBTQ stereotypes can often be very damaging to a queer individual just starting out in the world of work. For example, people may believe all queer people are active in pride rallies, that gay men dress in feminine or outrageous clothing, and that lesbians are always butch and dress like men. These are false stereotypes that can be misleading and cause confusion in the workplace. A female who prefers slacks to skirts and does not wear makeup or a male who is very expressive and dislikes sports may be treated unfairly when they do not adhere to typical gender stereotypes.

⅄ **Job Discrimination:** All of above barriers can lead to one single thing—job discrimination, a disparity in treatment of individual employees, based on their differences. Some bosses may be ashamed to promote or even hire LGBTQ people. One reason could be because they do not want to be associated with queer individuals. Another reason may involve the level of visibility the queer employee will have within the organization and with clients. Some managers may not want LGBTQ individuals to have roles that require a high level of visibility with clients because it may receive a negative reaction. As a result, queer employees may not be taken seriously in their careers or encounter a glass ceiling. While this attitude can be changed with hard work and education, for the most part it can make getting ahead difficult.

Queer Identity Development and Career Identity Development

Coming out in any environment is a personal choice. Just as coming out personally can be a challenging and difficult decision, so too is the decision to come out at the workplace. Personally, you may choose to come out to close friends and a few family members or you might decide to tell everyone. The same goes for coming out in the workplace. There are degrees of coming out you may consider; coming out to immediate coworkers and a supervisor or to the entire organization. It is important to remember that you probably will not come out just once at the workplace. As you meet new colleagues, clients, and move up in the organization you will be coming out all over again. This section establishes the link between coming out personally and professionally, examines the intersection of queer identity and career development, and evaluates the impact that one's overall queer identity may have.

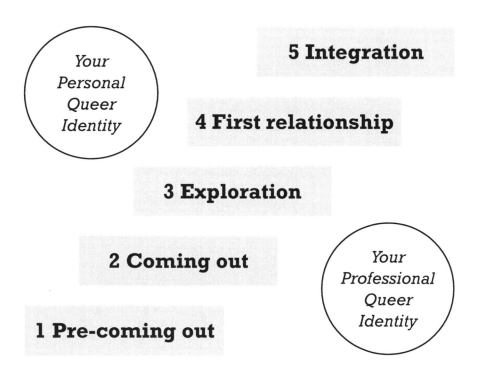

Figure 1: Overview of the five stages for the formation of a queer identity (Ref: Eli Colman Model)
{Generally used for personal queer identity, it is suggested that these stages can be adapted for when an individual enters the workplace as well.}

There are several models of queer identity formation; Cass, Coleman, Troiden, and Lipkin are probably the most well-known. This resource references Eli Colman's model[13]. This model contains five stages for the formation of a queer identity. See *Figure 1* for the overview of the five stages. As you read, identify the stage you feel that you are currently at personally and the path that lead you to that stage.

👤 SOMETHING TO THINK ABOUT

While queer identity development is usually discussed in stages, it can also be considered as a spectrum. It is important to remember that one's identity can change with such factors as time and experience.

Now that you have reviewed the stages and considered which stage you are at personally, let us look at the model from a career identity perspective. Career identity development involves self-realization that is achieved by integrating your career decision into your identity. This is done when people link their own motivations, interest, values, skills, and competencies to a career role.

It may be harder to do this as a queer person because so much attention has been spent on understanding your own sexual orientation or gender identity and less on your career identity. But this is where you need to be now. You cannot see your queer identity development and career identity development as two separate pieces. They need to converge.

---

13 E. Coleman, (1982). Developmental stages of the coming out process. Journal of Homosexuality, 7, 31-43.

In other words, at your identity synthesis stage, you need to incorporate the career identity development role into your life. Use your interests, skills, and values to find yourself a job that will be fulfilling and that will complement who you are as an out and proud member of the LGBTQ community.

Your queer identity can have an impact on your career development. Now let us explore the same model taking the career development into consideration. As you read through the stages, think about what stage you are at. The stage that you identified with personally may not be the equivalent when you apply it to the workplace. There is no one right way to walk your queer identity into the workplace. Again, I stress that it is a personal choice.

1. **Pre-coming out:** If you are at this stage personally and entering into the workplace at this stage, it can be a very difficult period. Not only are you trying to figure yourself out personally, you are thrown into an environment where you probably do not know many people, not aware of their views towards LGBTQ individuals, and where all you want to do is fit in. Individuals in the pre-coming out stage are at risk of negative career impacts because of a preoccupation with what is going on personally. It may affect their ability to concentrate or be productive. Not only is there a preoccupation with what is going on personally, but also with a concern of being discovered by colleagues. As mentioned earlier, in many states, it is still legal to fire someone solely based on their sexual orientation or gender identity. To counter these fears, one may elevate their straightness. This may involve even dating someone of the opposite sex just to keep a perceived image going. On the other end of the spectrum, people can retreat from participating in work/social activities

44

such as lunches or after hour gatherings due to fear that they could say something that might give them away. Somewhere in the middle, the new employee interacts on a limited basis, but switches pronouns when speaking about same sex persons of interest. All of these acts cannot only jeopardize productivity, but also cohesion among team coworkers and their direct supervisor.

2. **Coming out:** At this stage if the individual has had a positive experience in sharing her/his queer identity to close friends and family members, they are more willing to take that same approach to the workplace. This individual is more likely to tell colleagues within the same team or department and a direct supervisor. If that experience is positive, that circle will probably expand. Of course, one thing to consider is that your colleagues will talk with others. Therefore, you need to be prepared for more people at work to be in the know. This can actually take some of the pressure off you directly and work to your benefit.

3. **Exploration:** An individual at this phase has probably felt support from immediate colleagues and a supervisor. In addition, he or she probably has had a bit more time to understand the organization's culture. This can lead to individuals feeling comfortable being themselves and interacting with a broader range of employees, including other LGBTQ coworkers. At this stage, individuals begin to feel comfortable talking about their personal lives and showing pride in their queer identity. They may have a picture of their significant other in their cubical or invite their girlfriend/boyfriend to a social work event like a holiday party or happy hour.

4. **First relationship:** The first job after graduation can feel much like a first relationship. The impact of that experience can chart a path for years to come. In a negative situation, dealing with a hostile work environment can lead to a lack of productivity and a lack of self-worth. The individual is more likely to be distant with coworkers and spend time looking for a new job. In a positive situation, one can feel confident. The queer factor is less of an issue, and this individual is one moving more towards integration.

5. **Integration:** This is the stage when people can confidently bring their whole self to work, including their queer identity. There is a blending of one's personal and work identities, and life becomes harmonious. The individual has a greater ability to build and maintain relationships that will propel a career.

In summary, coming out occurs personally and professionally. Each of these processes can impact your career development. Identifying these stages can help you make better decisions when choosing the type of career you want to pursue and organizations that you would consider.

3 Exercises in Career Development

1. What stage on the identity model discussed are you at personally?

_____

_____

_____

1.1 What stage on the identity model discussed are you at professionally?

_____

_____

_____

1.2. Do you see this impacting your job search? Explain.

_____

_____

_____

2. *Rank the following values of importance to you.* *(1=lowest/ 5=highest)*

_____ Diversity

_____ High salary

_____ Inner harmony

_____ Prestige

_____ _____(*Insert your own value)

3. *What are the five barriers that can impact the career trajectory of LGBTQ people?*

_____

_____

_____

_____

A:

Homophobia

Perceived inappropriate job choices

Social stigmas

Stereotypes

Job discrimination

CHAPTER 3

Job Search Factors: Overview

Law and policy always involve compromise, and sometimes being a progressive means taking things one step at a time."

ZHOU DAN
(GAY, LAWYER,
CHINESE GAY PIONEER)

Once you have discovered or at least narrowed down your career choices, the next step is actively searching for an internship or job.

When looking for an internship, part-time job, or career after graduation you have a responsibility to research the organization before you complete an application or email your resume. The most basic question pertaining to LGBTQ inclusiveness you may want to investigate is whether or not the organization's equal employment opportunity statement/non-discrimination policy includes sexual orientation and gender identity.

Next, you may want to know if the organization offers domestic partner benefits. This can be deceptive. Many companies boast that they offer domestic partner benefits. However, a number of companies that offer such benefits will not pay the tax associated with the benefits for the domestic partner, leaving it to be deducted out of the employee's paycheck. This can be costly to the entry-level employee. This discrepancy does not occur for heterosexual couples.

Other topics include:

- ⋏ Whether the organization provides benefits such as relocation benefits and leave for domestic partners.
- ⋏ If sexual orientation and gender identity are addressed during diversity trainings.
- ⋏ Does the organization have an established LGBTQ employee resource group?

▲ Are gender-neutral restrooms available?

▲ Does the organization sponsor or participate in activities or events that support the LGBTQ community?

▲ Does the organization participate in recruiting events that target LGBTQ job seekers?

Understand What May Happen

It is clear that having a firm understanding of the issues is key to finding a great job. Along your journey there may be warning signs and barriers that you come across. It is recommended that you be prepared. Here are a few barriers you may experience:

▲ Rejection of your resume if you disclose your sexual orientation or gender identity.

▲ Outright rejection immediately after your interview if you disclose your sexual orientation/gender identity or are perceived to be an LGBTQ individual.

▲ You may be hired and then fired shortly after your sexual orientation or gender identity comes to light.

▲ You may experience immediate withdrawal, disapproval, or disgust from your coworkers if they find out that you are queer.

▲ Supervisors or coworkers might try to make you quit.

▲ You may experience harsh treatment, anger, or strong dislike from your boss or coworkers because of your sexual orientation or gender identity.

▲ You may get the job and find the social dynamics in the office or area extremely uncomfortable or even cruel.

TIP

If discrimination is something you have experienced, you may want to consider working for an LGBTQ-friendly company. These companies are supportive and non-discriminatory, which may make your life a lot easier.

These are just some of the things that may occur, which is why planning ahead is the best thing to do. You can avoid a lot of this opposition if you just do some basic investigation into the company in which you are applying. It is also vital that you know yourself and what you want as an employee at an organization.

Know Yourself and Your Career Path

If you are going to impress a potential employer, then you need to know yourself and what they want from you as an employee. Fortunately, because you are LGBTQ, you have had some unique character building experiences that your straight counterparts have not. These can be turned into strengths that can give you the edge over your competition. Knowing yourself will be a key component. This means being aware of the following:

1. **Know what you want**: You can remove a lot of trauma and hassle simply by knowing what you want out of a job. Finding out about the company and asking questions at the interview will tell you a lot about the

position you are applying. Create a list of your needs and see if that position meets them.

2. **Be aware of the warning signs:** If there are red flags when you begin the hiring process, then there may be red flags when you start working at the organization. If you experience discrimination or detect undertones of discrimination, feel discomfort, or pick up on any other form of anti-LGBTQ sentiment, consider not accepting the position.

3. **Identify barriers and overcome them:** Find out potential barriers to your employment and decide how to overcome them. For example, if your interviewer is homophobic and questions your experiences related to the LGBTQ community in a negative tone, how will you react?

In addition, consider your career path. Remember that your career is a collection of the positions that you choose. Your career is not your job! That is why knowing yourself is critical to the process. Then you can use your values, interests, and skills to create a process that you can use to find your ideal job. This will also be the basis for your career identity development.

Your sexual orientation/gender identity and your career identity need to be in harmony so that you can locate a position that will make you happy and play to your strengths. A good outcome is an office full of diverse people that do not discriminate—while you work hard on something that you love every day. A bad outcome is taking a job that you do not really want and being surrounded by ignorant people that dislike you because of your sexual orientation/gender identity—and they do not want you around. Being in a less-than-happy environment happens at times, which is why you need to make a conscious decision whether to stop the cycle of choosing such workplaces.

Gain Valuable Experience

There can be a vicious cycle when you are an LGBTQ person in the job market. Many jobs require you to have a certain amount of experience before you qualify for the position. As a member of the LGBTQ community, you may find yourself switching jobs often because your work environment was not a good fit. Or perhaps you were fired or mistreated. Either way, it is hard enough for a straight person to stay in one position long enough to gain experience, never mind someone with all the barriers you may face.

Remember any job that you accept should help you move towards your eventual career goal. That is what is called valuable experience. If you are taking any job you can find, even one that has nothing to do with your commitment of becoming, for example, a journalist, then you are expending time and energy on a role that is not moving you towards that goal.

 **SOMETHING TO THINK ABOUT**

Many feel that your sexual orientation/gender identity is your own business, and you can choose to share it or to keep it private at work. Keep in mind that your sexual orientation/ gender identity may prevent you from gaining valuable experience at certain companies that discriminate against LGBTQ people. In this instance, non-disclosure for a certain time may be something to consider.

Inclusive employers are not going to care about your sexual orientation/gender identity if you have the necessary knowledge, skills, and experience to add value to the job. However, if you work in a very conservative environment that demands a conservative nature—it may be unwise to disclose your sexual orientation/gender identity. If you are not a fairly open LGBTQ person, you may be able to get away with projecting a mainstream image, which may be an option for you. You should not have to hide who you are, but in some cases—it might be the only option if you want to get ahead in your career at a particular organization. Sometimes you will just have to decide what is more important: being out and open at work or gaining experience.

There are lines that you have to consider before you cross them. Everyone will be different. Some queer individuals may not be able to work without coming out to their coworkers. Then there will be some LGBTQ individuals that prefer not to share any personal information. It really is your call. As long as you are able to gain the valuable career experience you want and need, then anything goes. But think hard about the career choices that you make—you will have to live with them at the end of the day.

People in the Workplace

Once you have made the decision to join a chosen company —there is one skill that you need to become quite proficient at, and that is forming relationships with the people at work.

This cannot be stressed enough—real relationships break down prejudices and discrimination against LGBTQ people. When your coworkers and bosses get to know the real you, that is when you can really shine in your career. Building relationships is also an exceptional method of acclimatizing to the office vibe. Feel out the people you work for and work with. How do they feel about queer people? Is there an undercurrent of homophobia that runs through the workplace? Are there homophobic slurs being expressed?

You should be able to tell whether or not your office is the type of environment that will accept you as a queer person or not. It may be better to befriend a few people, and let them get to know you first, before dropping the news. If coworkers or supervisors ask you as a part of the casual office conversation, it is your choice whether to disclose your sexual orientation or gender identity. Realize there may be consequences either way. Simply hearing how your boss talks about a queer client and how colleagues treat other LGBTQ employees will give you insight into how they might react when they discover that you too identify as a queer individual.

FACT

Members of the LGBTQ community face high rates of workplace discrimination and harassment. Studies recently showed that as many as 43% of all gay[14] or transgendered people have experienced some form of extreme workplace discrimination.

It is important that you realize that you are probably not the first queer person hired by the organization. If there are other LGBTQ individuals in the office, seek them out and

14 Crosby Burns, Jeff Krehely, "Gay and Transgender People Face High Rates of Workplace Discrimination and Harassment," http://www.americanprogress.org/issues/lgbt/news/2011/06/02/9872/gay-and-transgender-people-face-high-rates-of-workplace-discrimination-and-harassment/

make friends with them! They probably have insight into understanding the office environment. Inquire whether the organization has an LGBTQ employee resource group. These groups generally have a business objective in which they serve the organization. However, they are also known to be a way to network and socialize with other queer employees and their allies. Relationships you make within the group could greatly benefit your career path.

If you hear that other LGBTQ employees have been discriminated against and mistreated, then you could always choose to look for another job or decide to keep your sexual orientation or gender identity private. This may allow you to gain valuable experience until another opportunity becomes available. It is suggested that you build real relationships and show everyone what a great employee you are. If they do eventually find out about your sexual orientation/gender identity, this may allow them to see past that part of you they struggle to understand.

Getting That Job

How do you actually land that ideal job? Well, it is always a good idea to understand what employers look for in candidates. Some of these attributes are listed below.

- **Interpersonal skills**: Connect well with others by being considerate, respectful, and helpful. People with great interpersonal skills work well in teams and are able to coordinate their activities with others better.
- **Strong work ethic**: Get down to business and you will be favored among others. A truly strong work ethic can accelerate a person's career significantly.
- **Great communication**: Employers want employees who can effectively communicate with individuals at

all levels of the organization. This is one skill that you cannot afford to leave off your list.

⅄ **Problem-solving ability**: The ability to see a problem, visualize the solution, articulate it, and solve the problem is a skill in high demand. The top managers in organizations are likely to be great problem solvers.

⅄ **Computer literate:** Do not just know the basics, be a computer whiz. Employees with strong computer skills are innovative, tech-smart, and sought after.

⅄ **Adaptability**: Be adaptable and open to change, and great things will happen for you in the workplace. An individual who is able to go with the flow and teach others how to do the same is always an asset.

⅄ **Team player**: Employers want individuals who work well with others, but have the ability to emerge as leaders. You may be a natural with people, but you will need to learn how to transition from team player to team leader.

Now review the list above and think if and how the attributes above, or others, have been shaped or enhanced as a result of your sexual orientation or gender identity. Consider these your 'G-assets' (gay assets). Next, think of an example or time that you have used the skill effectively. Finally, quantify or qualify the skill so that it is applicable to the position that you are seeking. These can be added to your resume or examples you provide at an interview.

For example, Jenna's experience of being out to some individuals and not to others about being a lesbian may have influenced the skill of adaptability. She demonstrated this skill in her previous position when asked to present a session on the state of the organization to senior level executives and another session on the same topic to the organization's line personnel. Jenna is currently applying to a marketing position where she would be responsible for writing and presenting copy to various clients.

4 Exercises in Job Search Factors

1. *List two red flags that you may encounter during your job search journey as an LGBTQ job seeker.*

   _____

   _____

   _____

2. *True or False. Relationship building in the workplace does not break down prejudices and discrimination in the workplace.*

   A: False

3. *Paul started working at an accounting firm immediately after graduating from college. He was never secretive about his sexual orientation, but he was not open about it either. Then one day he heard his boss telling a homophobic joke to a colleague. Paul realized at that point that he was working in an office with no discrimination policy in a state without any laws to protect him and was surrounded by potentially homophobic people. What should Paul do?*

a. Paul should find another job at a firm that respects people's rights.

b. Paul should confront his boss about the joke and come out to the office.

c. Paul should find out what his legal rights are, in case anyone finds out his secret.

d. Paul should continue working there and not say anything about his sexual orientation.

A: All can be correct to a degree. Explain your answer.

_____

_____

_____

4. *List an attribute discussed in this chapter and how it might have been shaped or enhanced as a result of your sexual orientation/gender identity. Next provide an example of using the skill effectively that you can use on a resume or at an interview*

_____

_____

_____

_____

_____

CHAPTER 4

Finding Successful Role Models & Mentors

If I had seen more people like me who are out and proud, it wouldn't have taken me 45 years to say it."

DON LEMON
(GAY, JOURNALIST,
NEWS ANCHOR)

Role models and mentors can be critical to an individual's career development. In the traditional sense, a role model is someone whose example, success, or behavior can be emulated by others. They are usually older and have established themselves in their careers. Role models can be anybody; including family members, friends, celebrities, sport figures, and business people. You may have a relationship with your role model or it is possible that you have never met him/her. A mentor is someone more skilled or experienced who can offer you advice, support, and guidance to facilitate the learning and development process. A mentor is someone who will make time to work with you as you build your career. Overtime, a mentee and mentor can form a lasting professional and personal relationship.

For an LGBTQ job seeker, role models and mentors that identify as LGBTQ can be someone to look up to, someone whom they can strive to be like in their careers or lives. Finding successful role models and mentors in the queer community is easy enough; you just need to know where to look. There are many associations and organizations that are packed with successful LGBTQ professionals willing to be a role models and mentors.

Who Is a Role Model to You?

Think about the attributes you look for in a role model. Often individuals are chosen to be role models because they demonstrate a passion for the work they do, live by a clear set of values, possess the ability to overcome obstacles, and exhibit a commitment to the larger community. Now think about role models you have currently or have had in the past. Identify who they are and what attributes they demonstrate.

Q FACT

A role model is someone you can look to for inspiration and support when you are facing problems at work. Their own stories may resonate with yours, casting light on your circumstances and guiding you to make more informed decisions.

Bandura's Social Learning Theory

"Individuals seek role models who are perceived as similar to them."
- Dr. Albert Bandura[15]

People learn from one another, through observation, modeling, and imitation. It is a completely natural process that occurs for everyone. Bandura's Social Learning Theory states that attention, memory, and motivation are all influenced by other people's actions in our own lives.

As you may have experienced, learning and development can be different for an LGBTQ person—as a child, at school, at college, and in the workplace. There is a significant social element to any sort of human development, something an LGBTQ person experiences differently. This is why many

---

15 Margaret Nauta, AmySaucier Leigh Woodard , Interpersonal Influences on Students Academic and Career Decisions: The Impact of Sexual Orientation, http://www. freepatentsonline.com/article/Career-Development-Quarterly/80746787.html

LGBTQ people seek out others in the queer community when they begin to accept their own sexual orientation and gender identity.

🔍 FACT

Albert Bandura's social learning theory stresses the importance of having good role models in your life to assist in personal development. This can be applied to queer identity and career development as well.

Bandura's social learning theory is based on three core factors —observation, reinforcement, and modeling.

1. The first is observation. An individual will learn how to behave based on what they perceive from influential people in their lives, such as parents and authority figures.
2. Next is intrinsic reinforcement, or a kind of internal reward for behaving a certain way.
3. Finally, there is modeling, which also involves attention, motivation, retention, and reproduction.

According to Bandura, people influence each other's beliefs, behaviors, and attitudes. This does not just happen in childhood; it happens during all stages of development—throughout a person's life. Finding a role model as a queer person is important for this very reason. If you do not surround yourself with supportive people who are able to guide you—either by inspiring you or directly helping you—then as an LGBTQ employee, you may struggle to find direction or satisfaction in your career.

What an LGBTQ Role Model Does

Aside from the fact that you will learn many great things from your LGBTQ role model, there are other reasons to invest yourself heavily into finding one you respect and admire. LGBTQ role models add real value to your life and your career. You may even consider having more than one role model.

According to Nauta, Saucier and Woodard[16,] role models may be able to assist with exemplifying how to stay true to who you are in the full context of a working environment. In addition, role models may be able to provide some perspective on combatting stereotypes of inappropriate and appropriate jobs for queer individuals.

🧑‍💼 SOMETHING TO THINK ABOUT

Consider having multiple role models. Have one or more from the LGBTQ community and one or more from the ally community. As a result, you will gain more than one source for inspiration and positive influence.

A considerable benefit associated with having LGBTQ role models is learning from their experiences and how they may have handled consequences and reactions after publically disclosing their sexual orientation or gender identity in the workplace. This can help prepare you for any kind of repercussions that may occur from your bosses

---

16   Margaret Nauta, Amy Saucier, Leigh Woodard, "Interpersonal Influences on Students Academic and Career Decisions: The Impact of Sexual Orientation," http://www.freepatentsonline.com/article/Career-Development-Quarterly/80746787.html

and colleagues. Keep in mind that these role models are people, and they can make mistakes or may opt to do things differently than you would.

It should be noted that allies of the LGBTQ community could also be great role models. These heterosexual individuals who support LGBTQ inclusion can play an important role in your career. Further, because they are outside of the LGBTQ community, they may offer a different perspective that you find beneficial.

Why You Need an LGBTQ Mentor

More than 75%[17] of all LGBTQ students consistently hear the terms 'faggot' or 'dyke' at school. This kind of emotional damage continues into college and into their careers. Having support from a mentor may mitigate some of the trauma associated with possible workplace issues. A very large part of self-actualization and skill development comes from searching for mentors that are like you. Consciously picking one or two may benefit your overall career progression.

There are many great reasons why you need a queer mentor in your career. Aside from the many valuable insights this person will be able to give you, here are few queer specific reasons:

- ⅄ An LGBTQ mentor is someone you can confide in about how it feels to be who you are at work (out and proud or not willing to disclose your sexual orientation and gender identity).

- ⅄ Your queer mentor can be a great critic, who can keep you honest or tell you when you have overstepped

---

17 John R Selig, Role Models For Gay Youth in America Can Be a Matter of Life of Death, http://www.johnselig.com/commentary/gayyouth/

the mark on a personal and professional level. Work/life balance can be a challenge for those new to the workplace.

▲ Your LGBTQ mentor can be connected to many other professionals in the LGBTQ community. He or she can introduce you to people and help you build connections with the right people in your field.

▲ Your queer mentor can help you deal with discrimination issues if they happen to arise at work. You will be able to discuss whether or not what occurred was in fact discrimination and possible actions to take.

▲ Your LGBTQ mentor can help you define your goals and will make sure that you are working towards them. He or she will help you be accountable and responsible for your own actions and the future of your career.

▲ Your queer mentor is a constant ally in an environment that may not encourage queer culture. The job market can be brutal, and getting ahead can be equally as tough —more so when you are dealing with the complexities of being an LGBTQ employee.

You need your very own queer mentor because there may

FACT

A queer mentor in your life can equip you with valuable insight and knowledge into the business world and how to get ahead there. They have faced the unique challenges you may face and have overcome them.

be challenges in the workplace you cannot work through with your straight colleagues. Instead of feeling misunderstood, isolated, or confused, you will have your mentor to make sure that you are enlightened and pro-active.

Aligning Your Goals with Your Mentor

It is always a good idea to try to choose an LGBTQ mentor who has worked in a similar field in which you have interest. That way, you not only get the benefit of your mentor's queer knowledge, you get his or her actual work knowledge as well.

Choosing a mentor who can help you on your career path all depends on your goals. If it is your goal, for example, to eventually become a manager of the company that you are working for—then you may want to find a mentor who is currently a manager. Also consider having more than one mentor. Perhaps you can learn a lot from the sales manager, and combine that with the information and counsel you get from another manager—such as an operations manager.

All mentors should be accomplished in their careers so that they are equipped to provide you with advice. In addition, mentors should be great at teaching you valuable lessons by speaking to you about what they have experienced in their careers. It is common that mentors are older than their mentees. For those individuals transitioning from academia to the workplace, a mentor who can shed light on the experiences they had during the same process could be of significant value.

Before you find yourself a mentor, queer or not, make a list of the character traits that you admire in people who hold leadership positions in your field. When you can find an LGBTQ mentor that fits this profile, then you are on your way!

Being a mentee is all about allowing self-improvement in your career. If you make it a priority, then you will honestly benefit from it for many years. While discrimination and problems mainly rise at the beginning or end of jobs, or at periods of advancement, there is no reason why a mentor cannot help you through it all. Align your goals with your mentor, and you will have a reliable resource that you can tap into whenever you need. That is progressive career advancement.

3 Exercises in Finding a Role Model/Mentor

1. *List the core personality traits that you admire in a role model.*

_____

_____

_____

_____

_____

_____

_____

2. *Natalie was up for a promotion at work when she overheard some hurtful comments about her ongoing gender transitioning process coming from a colleague's office. She became worried that she would lose the promotion because of this reaction to her gender identity status in the workplace. What questions could she ask her mentor in order to put her mind at ease?*

---

3. *Circle the characteristics you look for in a mentor.*
   a. Wealthy
   b. Respected in their area of work
   c. At the top of their field
   d. Successful LGBTQ employee at work
   e. A good teacher
   f. Older and wiser
   g. Active in LGBTQ networking associations
   h. Has dealt with discrimination before
   i. Able to spend some time with you
   j. Gives great advice about being out in the workplace
   k. Knowledgeable in your area of focus
   l. Is who or where you'd like to be

   3.1. Are there other attributes you seek? List them.

CHAPTER 5

Your LGBTQ Inclusive Employers

Nothing strengthens authority so much as silence."

LEONARDO DA VINCI
(GAY, ARTIST, INVENTOR, SCIENTIST)

At some point in the job seeking process everyone faces the question, what sort of working environment will I be happy in? This basic question can mean something deeper for queer job seekers. Will I be accepted? Will I be safe? That is why you need to decide whether each potential job will be a good organizational fit for you. Will you insist on LGBTQ friendly companies? Will you lean towards LGBTQ friendly companies but not mind if they do not meet the requirements? Or will you consider all organizations no matter what their level of LGBTQ inclusion may be?

Why LGBTQ-Inclusive Employers?

An LGBTQ-inclusive employer is one that protects lesbian, gay, bisexual, transgender, and queer people from discrimination while on the job. Further, LGBTQ-inclusive employers tend to hire people who are fair and accepting of a diverse workplace. It is important to consider whether you will look exclusively for employment opportunities with organizations that are LGBTQ-inclusive or whether you are open to work for an employer that does not promote workplace equality for LGBTQ individuals.

While there may always be those few who are not accepting, working for a business that encourages diversity and has actually written it into business policy is good for you. That way if discrimination occurs, you can report to the proper individuals in the company with less fear of retaliation.

> ## 👤💭 SOMETHING TO THINK ABOUT
>
> Your work environment can affect your work performance and job satisfaction. A higher level of job satisfaction and performance means that you will likely progress in your career faster, while the opposite can occur if you choose to ignore the impact of a work environment.

Usually queer inclusive employers appreciate, recognize, and happily tap into the perspectives and insights that a diverse employee base has to offer. They promote innovation and collaboration in addition to focusing on high levels of productivity and valuing input from all employees. The opposite of this is a business that does not have a firm policy on LGBTQ discrimination. You may need to be careful at these organizations, and tread lightly because no policy protects your employment the company.

How to Find These Employers

Naturally, for a queer employee who wants to be accepted by colleagues and bosses, LGBTQ-inclusive organizations may be preferred to others. Just the fact that the employer is LGBTQ-inclusive means that you are likely to find other LGBTQ employees working at the company—which is great news for you! As such, these employers are in demand by LGBTQ job seekers. Finding these employers is not difficult if you know where to look. However, depending on your field, there may be many or very few of them.

Job Postings

Employers that promote diversity in the workplace are usually proud to be inclusive, and they advertise that fact in their job postings. Look for clues that may indicate your potential employer wants diversity in the business. For example, if the organization's non-discrimination policy inclusive of gender identity and sexual orientation is included in the job posting.

> ## TIP
>
> Search online for an employer's non-discrimination policy. Look for telling language—such as Company X follows an equal opportunity employment policy and employs personnel without regard to race, creed, color, ethnicity, national origin, religion, sex, sexual orientation, gender expression, age, physical or mental ability, veteran status, military obligations, and marital status.

Online Lists

There are LGBTQ-friendly websites that host a database of companies and information about their employment policies and practices. Many of these databases have a handy search function so you can plug in a company name and find their website or a copy of their policy. For example, the Human Rights Campaign (HRC) releases a *Best Places to Work for LGBTQ Individuals* list. Click on an organization such as American Airlines and see a summary of the policies and benefits that the company offers to LGBTQ employees.

Search Engines

Use Google or one of the other search engines to try and find companies in your area that are looking to hire with diversity in mind. Use specific keyword phrases such as employee policy, equal opportunity, or code of ethics to find their hiring policies.

LGBTQ Websites

LGBTQ equality in the workplace is a hot topic. Individuals and organizations have taken the time to create helpful websites that you can visit and find accurate information about your field. For example, those seeking a career in law can check out the National LGBT Bar Association webpage. Most of these websites have search filters and other resources that you can use to get in touch with the right people. Borngay.procon.org for example has numerous lists and search functions you can use to get hold of the right information. Often these LGBTQ websites will also promote certain organizations or associations where you can meet many contacts and expand your career by networking with people in the LGBTQ community.

The HOT List and the CEI

One of the most useful lists that you can get hold of is the *HOT List*. It stands for "Hiring Out Talent" and is produced by OUT for Work, a national nonprofit organization that is dedicated to educating, preparing, and empowering LGBTQ job seekers. The *HOT List* has been popular since it was released in 2007, and is a detailed index of organizations with excellent LGBTQ-inclusive policies and that are currently hiring people.

According to OUT for Work, LGBTQ inclusion policies and current hiring levels are the two most important criteria for any LGBTQ person searching for a job. The *HOT List* uses information from a number of sources in its evaluation. Each organization is evaluated on two primary components; the anticipated number of entry-level hires they anticipate for the year and on how inclusive their workplace equality practices are for LGBTQ employees. In true style, the ratings start at "Hot", and then improve to "Hotter" and finally "Burning Hot". In 2008, only 16 companies made it onto the "Burning Hot" list out of 123 LGBTQ friendly companies included in the publication.

The *Corporate Equality Index* (CEI) is also an excellent place to source LGBTQ-friendly employers. It is the national benchmarking tool on corporate policies and practices related to LGBTQ employees. The index was launched in 2002 by the Human Rights Campaign (HRC) and has become one of the leading roadmaps for LGBTQ job seekers looking for safe employment. The *CEI* aspires to be fair, transparent, and rigorous, and aims to identify employers and emerging employer's practices that improve LGBTQ employees' experience at work.

The index is based on responses provided by organizations that complete the survey. The rating criterion includes evaluation of the company's equal employment opportunity policy, employment benefits, organizational LGBT competency, public engagement, and responsible citizenship. Companies receive a score of 0-100%. Results of the *CEI* can be found in print or online at hrc.org[18]. In fact, the HRC website offers a convenient search mechanism consisting of all the organizations that have completed the survey. All you need

---

18 Corporate Equality Index, Human Rights Campaign, http://www.hrc.org/corporate-equality-index#.UOXH7W_296w

to do is type in the organization's name and their score along with other valuable information is revealed.

There are other resources on the HRC website, including responses from businesses that made it onto the index or that managed to achieve a 100% rating. These are nice to read, especially if you are considering a career at one of these organizations.

It should be noted that statistics from the 2013 report state that 99%[19] of America's *Fortune 500* companies that participated in the survey have non-discrimination policies in regards to sexual orientation. Further, 83% of the same *Fortune 500* companies that completed the survey have non-discrimination policies based on gender identity. Further, 94% of these organizations provided domestic partner benefits and 41% provide trans-inclusive benefits.

Diversity Inc. Magazine and Company Websites

Diversity Inc. magazine is a prominent magazine that has devoted itself to promoting diversity and educating people on the merits of diversity in the workplace. The magazine publishes five times a year, but also offers online resources. The initiatives of *Diversity Inc.* magazine have contributed to many companies drafting their own diversity policies, including those that level the playing field for LGBTQ individuals.

Besides bringing a wide variety of tools, resources, and information to individuals and businesses alike, *Diversity Inc.* is well known for its Top 50 Companies for Diversity list.

With more than 500 companies actively participating in the survey, it is no wonder this list is one of the more exclusive and desirable lists to be on. According to *Diversity*

---

19   CEI, http://www.hrc.org/corporate-equality-index/#.UMgjBYP29ic

Inc., the proper use of diversity management means the proactive management of sexual orientation, gender identity, culture, race, age, and disability to ensure equal outcome in workplace relationships. There are a number of unique awards that they hand out each year to companies that excel at diversity management. The list you may want to focus on is the *Diversity Inc. Top 10 Companies for LGBT Employees.*

Another way of finding out if a company has equal opportunity policies or is an LGBTQ-inclusive employer is to look on their website. The fastest way to access their employee policies is to find their site map and quickly glance through their site, looking for specific phrases that may indicate that you have found the right area.

If that does not work, then use the search bar located at the top of these websites in the header area. Simply type LGBTQ or employee policy to locate the right pages. If the site has a career section, you can also look there. Often when a company is proud of their diversity and progressive policies, they will announce it either by placing an icon on their site or mentioning it in their description on the page. For example, IBM proudly displays that it is included in *Diversity Inc.'s Top 50 Companies for Diversity* on their webpage.

🔍 FACT

The *Diversity Inc. Top 10 Companies for LGBT Employees* is one of the premier lists for finding quality employers. Each year, companies go through a stringent survey process. If a company makes the list, it exemplifies that they are leaders in creating LGBTQ-inclusive work environments.

Trade Magazines, Events, Associations

One of the other ways of locating LGBTQ-inclusive employers is by getting your hands on trade magazines. A good example is *Accounting Today*, the long-time trade magazine for accountants. If there is a trade, there is at least one trade magazine available. This is especially true of the analytical fields such as law, medicine, and science. However, there is also a current boom in technology trade magazines that you should look into if this is your field. These trade magazines publish articles on LGBTQ issues and diversity, produce best-of lists, and advertise job opportunities.

Another way to find queer inclusive employers is to attend LGBTQ community events in your area. Networking events or events supporting the LGBTQ community are excellent opportunities. Pride events, walks, fundraising events, and gala dinners that support the LGBTQ community are just a few examples of events that may be taking place near you. Even if you cannot attend, take a look at website and marketing materials. Take note of the companies supporting the event. This is a clear indication of their support of the LGBTQ community.

If you can attend an event, use the opportunity to network. It is probably not the best idea to unload all your questions on someone that you meet at such an event. However exchange contact information and be sure to follow up with an email. The person you meet might not know the answers to the questions you might have, however, they can surely connect you with someone that does.

What is the best resource available? Current employees! While lists and publications highlight LGBTQ-inclusiveness, there is no better source about what the real environment is like than someone who is working in it. You may have an opportunity to meet individuals at community events, career fair, through a career center, or through friends and family members.

It is important to understand that your first point of contact may not provide you with the information you are seeking, however, they can direct you to others within the organization. For example, you may be able to set up an informational interview with a representative from the human resources department or a meeting with a member of the LGBTQ employee resource group.

> ## TIP
>
> It is always a good idea to do as much research as possible into the job opportunities that you explore. Finding an LGBTQ-friendly company now can make a real difference in your career in the long term. Better references, working environments, leadership opportunities, and benefits matter.

Attending these community events can put you in touch with employees that already work at LGBTQ-friendly companies. From there you can get a direct personal reference from these individuals, which will help you scope out companies in your area of interest.

You will also need to get in touch with employees outside of events. If you are truly interested in a job position, but you cannot find much about the company online, or there is just a general absence of LGBTQ information—it is best to get in contact with an employee. Ask them questions that will help you better understand how that company treats LGBTQ employees. This sort of first person perspective is necessary if you cannot find out anything about that company online. At least you have some valuable knowledge before the interview.

Finally, get in touch with your local LGBTQ associations. They will have ample resources available. Better yet, leverage their connections with local businesses. Reaching out to associations may seem quite daunting, but they can be really helpful. An example is the National Gay and Lesbian Chamber of Commerce (NGLCC), a nonprofit organization that acts as the direct link between LGBT business owners, corporations, and government. Under the umbrella organization are affiliate organizations throughout the country. These affiliates serve the same mandate at the local level. For organizations that might be small to medium in size or not included in many publications, this may be a good starting point for your investigation.

5 Exercises in Finding LGBTQ Employers

1. *Go online and list at least three trade magazines that may help you explore organizations for internship and job opportunities.*

   1)

   2)

   3)

2. *Found an organization? Run through this handy LGBTQ inclusion checklist.*

   - What LGBTQ or diversity lists are they on?
   - Is sexual orientation included in the organization's non-discrimination policy?
   - Is gender identity included in the organization's non-discrimination policy?
   - Does the organization provide domestic partner benefits?
   - Does the organization provide other benefits, such as relocation benefits, leave, etc. for same-sex partners as they do for married couples?
   - Does the organization facilitate diversity training that includes sexual orientation and gender identity?
   - Is there an LGBTQ employee resource group?
   - Does the organization have at least one gender neutral restroom?
   - Does the organization sponsor or participate in activities or events that support the LGBTQ community?
   - Does the organization participate in recruiting events that target LGBTQ candidates?

2.1. *Do the answers collectively persuade you whether you would work for the organization or not? Explain.*

_____

_____

_____

2.2. *Are there any specific questions on the checklist that concern you more than others? If so, which ones?*

_____

_____

_____

3. *Garrett is a job seeker who identifies as gay. He wants to find a job at a prominent - though LGBTQ-inclusive - technology firm. He is highly qualified and has experienced some discrimination in the workplace before due to his sexual orientation, which is part of the reason why he is now seeking a company with an LGBTQ policy. What advice would you give Garrett on how to find a tech firm that values diversity, equality, and LGBTQ employees in the workplace?*

_____

_____

_____

_____

_____

4. *List three organizations that traditionally hire individuals with your discipline and that are considered LGBTQ-inclusive.*

   1.

   2.

   3.

5. *Where can you find LGBTQ employers in your area?*
   a. LGBTQ associations and organizations
   b. By networking online
   c. Public events
   d. All of the above

   A: d

CHAPTER 6

Creating Your Resume

I had to come out because it was too hard not being myself."

KYE ALLUMS
(TRANSGENDER, ATHLETE)

Resume writing is a discipline all its own. Do it well and it can catapult you ahead of all other applicants. Do a poor job of creating your resume and it will probably end up in the trash folder. Crafting a good resume can be cumbersome, but the reward will be an interview.

You may be thinking, so what does that have to do with my sexual orientation and gender identity? When talking about coming out on your resume, it is not about announcing that you are queer in bold courier font or printing it out on rainbow colored paper. The issue is whether or not to include information on your resume that directly associates you with the LGBTQ community. Deciding to be out on your resume will be impacted by many variables including where you are on the queer identity continuum discussed earlier.

Queer applicants have extra concerns when creating a resume. For example:

- Do you disclose that you are a member of an LGBTQ association?
- Do you include one of your achievements such as receiving an award from an LGBTQ organization?
- Do you include work experience with an LGBTQ advocacy organization?

What to Put on Your Resume

Deciding what information to include on a resume for heterosexuals can be daunting. If you are a queer jobseeker, that decision can even be more challenging. Based on the descriptions, details, and inclusions you choose to present on your resume—the employer will decide whether or not to take it a step further and invite you to an interview. Remember the ONLY purpose that a resume has in the job search process is to get you that interview opportunity.

It is important to remember that the resume is not your life story. Your resume needs to be concise, simple, and impressive. In regards to work experience, only include information that strengthens your chance to obtain the interview. The rest you can leave off. For some reason, people feel the need to include every place that they worked on their resume. This is generally frowned upon.

FACT

A resume is the first impression that a company has of you, so it needs to be professional—it should be written and edited with strategic information and formatted in a presentable, modern way. Often what distinguishes applicants from each other are the basic aesthetics of a resume.

In addition, you cannot create a one-size-fits-all resume. You can however have a base template. Just be sure to optimize it to suit the purposes and needs of the position that you are applying. When employers see stock resumes or ones that are tacky, messy, or long they may become frustrated. As a result, your resume could end up in the do-not-call pile.

Should You Be Out and Open?

One of the most common questions that an LGBTQ applicant asks is, "Should I be out and open on my resume?" It is not a small question, as impressions are made pretty quickly with resumes.

Should you include *LGBTQ* activities and affiliations on your resume?

The only answer here is: *it depends*. If the company that you are applying to is an LGBTQ-friendly company, then maybe you should. If it is a conservative organization where this may be seen as a negative on your resume and could prevent you from being invited for an interview—maybe you should leave it out.

ALWAYS consider your audience. Who is likely to be screening or reading your resume? Will it be an HR professional who has had training in inclusive hiring practices, or a department manager who may be great at the work they do, but lacks the skillset involved in interviewing compliance? If possible do some research and find out. It will give you the upper hand.

TIP

If you have chosen not to come out on your resume, you can consider including your experience with LGBTQ organizations by referring to them as diversity, community, or minority associations. This will allow you to include all of your work-orientated skills, duties, and talents with less fear of potential discrimination.

ALWAYS consider how relevant it is to list your LGBTQ experiences, associations, or affiliations on your resume. If you are a lawyer, it may be a big plus to include your participation in an LGBTQ law association's activities and other events. In contrast, an activity such as participating in the local AIDS walk may not be as relevant.

Before you decide to be out and open about your affiliations, ask yourself these questions:

- ⅄ Do they enhance or highlight your skills, abilities, or talents?
- ⅄ Do they count as valuable work experience?
- ⅄ Do they cast you in a positive light?

How to Include It in Your Resume

If you answered no to any of the above questions, then perhaps you should refrain from adding such content. Remember the goal here is to get the interview. If you answered yes, then ask yourself; will I feel comfortable speaking about the LGBTQ associations presented on my resume when I get the interview? This falls back to where you are personally and professionally in your queer identity and career development.

If you have decided to be out and open on your resume there are various ways you can do so. You will need to consider how you present this information because that is just as important as deciding to include it in your resume. There are many ways to add skills, abilities, and talents to your resume that fit your personal and professional comfort level. First, you could choose to spell out lesbian, gay, bisexual, transgender, and queer on your resume when referring to organizations.

Example: Vice president of the lesbian, gay, bisexual,

transgender, queer, and ally student campus group

If you are not comfortable with that, you can use the acronym, LGBTQA.

Example: Vice president of the LGBTQA student campus group

If that is also uncomfortable, you can always use neutral phrases such as diversity or minority group. Or you can add the specific name of the student organization.

Example: Vice president of the diversity student campus group

Example: Vice president of Spectrum

Another factor to consider is your audience; not only the industry, the organization, but the individual as well. If your potential employer is a well-known LGBTQ-friendly employer, then you probably do not have to worry as much about the way you present your sexual orientation/gender identity on your resume. Most likely someone from the human resources department will screen your resume and therefore it is less likely to be tossed aside because of your queer professional experiences. If you are fortunate enough to know the person who will be reviewing resumes, for example if it is someone you met at a career fair, that too could influence the wording that you use.

Finally, at some point your resume will probably leave the hands of a trained HR professional and into those of a manager or supervisor. This is where someone's personal negative bias towards individuals that identity as LGBTQ may impact the process. Remember that you have to be willing to talk about everything you have listed on your resume at the interview confidently and in a convincing way.

Including your sexual orientation or gender identity on

TIP

Before submitting your resume it is always a good idea to have another set of eyes look at it. If you are concerned about the queer-related content, ask someone who is LGBTQ and someone who is straight to review your resume. Get honest opinions from both of them and make the necessary adjustments.

your resume is a personal decision. If you want to keep it private, then omitting all details is probably the best thing to do. Accurate research and good decisions about where you want to work and whom you want to work with also make a difference!

Tips on Great Resume Creation

To create an excellent resume, you need to lay out a plan according to the job position that you are applying for. Every single resume must be specifically written to the job description. People that screen resumes can tell if yours is a bulk, template resume that you have sent to numerous companies.

- If possible, find out the name of the person whom you are sending your resume to and use this in your cover letter. A cover letter needs to be the motivation for your resume—in other words, why you are applying for that specific position at that company.
- Always do your homework on the company. Find out

exactly what the job description is and streamline your resume to fit into this exact mold. List the associations or attributes that make you the best candidate. Research is the key to all successful resumes.

▲ You may be an LGBTQ applicant, but it is important to sell that you are the best applicant for the job. It is nice that you have come out on your resume, but if you do not have the answer to the interviewer's eternal question —why should he/she entertain the idea of hiring you for the position, you are less likely to get the job.

▲ Have your resume written, edited, and formatted by a professional. Use a local college career center or an outsourcing service. They will ensure that you do not have any grammatical errors, issues, or formatting trouble when they open your resume. If it is a digital version, use Microsoft Word or make it a PDF file.

▲ If you do not want to be out on your resume, remember to exclude any organizations or associations that are LGBTQ in nature.

Use these tips to create a tailored resume that is perfect for the job position. Remember, aside from the LGBTQ content, if it does not make you look good, do not include it in your resume. Align yourself with the position that you are applying for —always mention work experience and why it RELATES to your current application.

The Pros and Cons of LGBTQ Content on Resumes

There are pros and cons that you will have to weigh when creating your resume. These will need to be reviewed each time you prepare to send a resume.

The Pros

⏶ Being out on your resume by listing your professional experience and involvement within the LGBTQ community can add value to why a company should hire you. If you leave the skills or experiences off your resume, you can be putting yourself at a disadvantage.

⏶ Being honest about your association and experience with the LGBTQ community may lead to employment because your potential employer wants to expand the diversity in the company or its client base. In this instance, it is an asset to come out on your resume.

⏶ If you are out on your resume and you get the interview, you can feel confident speaking about those LGBTQ affiliations during the interview with less fear of being discriminated against.

👤💭 SOMETHING TO THINK ABOUT

Whether it is fair or not—people may judge you based on your sexual orientation/gender identity when you include it on your resume. Always do your homework on the organization's LGBTQ inclusiveness. Also consider your level of comfort with discussing your professional experiences in the LGBTQ community that relate to the position.

The Cons

⏶ Coming out on your resume by listing your involvement with LGBTQ associations may lead your potential employer to think that you are a radical—leading gay pride rallies, being overly sensitive about who you are, and making trouble for those around you who are not accepting. For this reason, they could avoid you.

⋏ You never know who is screening resumes at corporations or firms these days. Even if that person does not hold a position of power, he or she could be extremely prejudiced against LGBTQ individuals. If this happens, one person may discard your resume— not giving you a chance to join what is actually a really inclusive working environment.

⋏ Being out on your resume may overshadow your education, skills, talents, and attributes, leading to rejection. The person reviewing the resume may not be overtly biased or prejudiced, but subconsciously values your skills less than someone else's because of your sexual orientation and gender identity.

Resumes for Those with Limited Professional Experience

Many college students think that they do not have enough experience to create a resume. For most, this assumption is false. It may be true that college students do not have much actual work experience, however recruiters already know that. They are likely to focus on other sections of your resume in order to get a better understanding of your educational background, skills, and experiences. Sections may include projects, leadership, membership, honors, achievements, activities and interests, and community/volunteer activities. Here are examples of these sections containing LGBTQ related content presented in various ways:

Projects: This section of the resume is where you can highlight your knowledge with experiences outside a job or internship. You can include academic projects/papers on your resume to highlight class experiences and knowledge that may be relevant to an employer.

- ▲ Participated in marketing class projects, including developing a comprehensive marketing plan for local minority focused nonprofit organization

  This example uses the term minority to describe the type of LGBTQ nonprofit organization.

Leadership: You can list the leadership positions that you have held in campus organizations. Stressing accomplishments under your leadership is encouraged.

- ▲ Gay Straight Alliance, Penn State University
- ▲ Vice President (1/11-1/12)
- ▲ Organized venues and transportation for all programmatic efforts
- ▲ Managed $3,000 budget

  This example directly associates you with the LGBTQ community.

Memberships: Include memberships in professional organizations that you are involved or hold leadership positions.

- ▲ CAGLCC, Student Member, 2010 – Present

  CAGLCC is the acronym for the Capital Area Gay and Lesbian Chamber of Commerce. You may be asked to explain the acronym.

Honors: Your academic honor societies, scholarships, and awards can be highlighted in this section of your resume.

- ▲ Point Foundation Scholarship Recipient, Fall 2011

*The Point Foundation provides financial support to students who are marginalized due to sexual orientation, gender identity or gender expression.

Achievements: Accomplishments demonstrate that you have the ability to produce positive results and achieve success. They give potential employers the confidence to know that you will be successful in the position.

⋏ Developed and implemented new student outreach program, which expanded membership in campus diversity group by 35%

*This example eliminates direct LGBTQ reference. You may or may not be asked about the diversity group.

Activities & Interests· This section is where you can list student organizations, professional associations, and committees that you have participated. More than just listing these, you will want to highlight your involvement and leadership positions that you held.

⋏ Spectrum, Louisiana State University

⋏ Technology/Web Committee (9/11-5/12)

⋏ Created and administered student survey assessing the technological needs of the group

⋏ Facilitated PowerPoint presentation based on results of survey to group leadership, faculty, and staff.

*The name of the LGBTQ group in this example is Spectrum. There is no direct reference to the group being LGBTQ in nature.

Community Involvement/Volunteer Activities: This shows that the job applicant is a well- rounded individual who cares deeply about community. It is recommended that you indicate any achievements that resulted as your volunteer efforts.

- ▲ AIDS Walk 2010
- ▲ August 2010 – October 2010
- ▲ Responsibilities: Coordinated outreach and fundraising efforts of 50 member Lesbian, Gay, Bisexual, Transgender, and Ally campus team

  This shows more than the fact that you participated in the walk. It also directly associates you with the LGBTQ community.

Remember, the sole purpose of your resume is to land an interview. Consider each piece of information and what you know about who will be screening resumes and selecting who to interview. It is important to be strategic with what information you include on your resume and how you include it.

4 Exercises to Complete a Successful Resume

1. Provide three reasons why an LGBTQ job seeker would want to be out on a resume?

    1.

    2.

    3.

2. Name three things that you should always do when preparing a successful resume.

    _____

    _____

    _____

    _____

    _____

3. Why is it important to have a resume strategy?

    _____

    _____

    _____

    _____

    _____

4. *Chance is considering sending his resume in response to an events manager position at a globally recognized hotel chain. In addition to holding various professional positions in event management, he also was the chair for the statewide LGBTQ Equality Dinner for two years. He is not sure if he should include the information on his resume considering he has been out of work for almost nine months due to downsizing at his last organization. What advice would you give Chance? What can he do in advance of sending his resume?*

CHAPTER 7

Being Successful at Interviews

*There will not be a
magic day when we
wake up and it's now
OK to express ourselves
publicly. We make
that day by doing
things publicly until
it's simply the way
things are."*

TAMMY BALDWIN
(LESBIAN,
POLITICAL FIGURE)

Finding a great company to apply to can be tough enough, then you have to get past the resume process—and you will have to ace the interview if you want the job. This is the final stage in securing the job that you want.

When talking about coming out at the interview, it is not about shaking the interviewer's hand and announcing that you are gay, lesbian, bisexual, transgender, or queer. The idea is deciding whether or not to speak about experiences that are directly associated with the LGBTQ community. The answer will be impacted by many variables. Primarily, did you present such experiences on the resume, that now sits in the hands of the interviewer across the table from you?

It is important to understand that anything you put on your resume is fair game for the interviewer to ask you to explain in further detail. You have to be able to speak confidently and convincingly in the interview. An interview can be a stressful situation; any stumble or hesitation could jeopardize you getting an offer.

For the queer job seeker, there are additional issues that arise—should you come out at the interview? Why do you want to come out? When is a good time to do so? How do you come out in a professional manner?

Should You Come Out in the Interview?

As a point of reference, it is important to reflect on where you fall on the queer identity model as it relates to your career development.

The first thing you need to consider is what your interview strategy is going to be. Coming out at the interview is solely your choice—but if you decide to do it you will need a plan. The process can go one of four ways.

1. If you came out on your resume, then be prepared to talk about your skills, talents, and abilities associated with your involvement in LGBTQ associations and professional experiences at the interview. Interviewers are obligated to explore all parts of a resume, and if you included it on your resume you can expect questions about it.

2. If you chose not to come out on your resume and plan to use the interview itself as an opportunity to test the waters, then prepare when and how. For example, when an employer asks if you have any questions, you may want to ask about leadership opportunities outside of the primary role such as participating in an employee resource group (ERG). Asking which groups they have or if they have an LGBTQ-specific group is an option. Additionally, you could let the interviewer know that you held a leadership position within your LGBTQ campus/community group and would be interested in getting involved in the employee resource group.

3. If you have decided not to come out at the interview, that is perfectly fine. It could be that your LGBTQ experiences are not relevant to the position for which you are applying.

4. A key to good interviewing is being prepared. Having thought out responses to commonly asked questions can really help you land the job—especially if you are put on the spot. Interviews are stressful enough without having to figure out how to explain something on

your resume about an LGBTQ affiliation to a complete stranger.

> ## 🔍 FACT
>
> Seeking employment at a company with a diverse workforce will make the interview process or coming out a lot easier. Chances are, the interviewer has knowingly and unknowingly interviewed queer candidates before. The key here is to be professional and focus on your talents and skills!

How to Come Out in an Interview

If you decide to come out during the interview, knowing how to do so is obviously the next challenge. It is important that you do not make the entire interview about your sexual orientation/gender identity.

Incorporate it into the normal flow of the interview

You can be assured that an interviewer will ask you about skills that you possess.

"My ability to multi-task is a skill I am confident will benefit the organization. In addition to taking a full academic course load and working a part-time job, I was also a representative on student government and the public relations chair for the LGBTQ campus group on campus."

Wait until the Q&A at the end of the interview

The interviewer may start talking about the benefits offered by the company towards the end of the interview.

"Does the organization offer domestic partner benefits?"

It should be noted that domestic partner benefits are also offered to heterosexual couples that are not married. As a result this would not always signal the rainbow flag.

🖊️ TIP

Your interview needs to be mainly about what academic, personal, or professional experiences make you qualified for that position. You need to focus on WHY you are the best for that job, and you can use your LGBTQ affiliations to bolster this.

Ask a question about diversity in the workplace.

"Would you say that the company has a diverse employee base?"

If you have included queer professional experiences or associations in your resume, be prepared to answer questions about it.

Interviewer: *"I see that you won the Out in Leadership Award from the Lavender Professional Association of Arizona? Tell me more about that."*

You: *"Yes, the award is presented to one individual a year for their academic and philanthropic achievements within the lesbian, gay, bisexual, transgender, and queer community. I was recognized for my 4.0 GPA and work on organizing and managing all aspects of a local grassroots campaign of $100,000 and 250 individuals on the defeat the state's proposed ban on gay marriage."*

Whatever your answer, always make yourself look good – without boasting. Be confident and friendly, and maintain eye contact with your interviewer. If you become embarrassed or flustered over the subject that your interviewer brings up, it can steer the interview in a bad direction.

Preparation and Research

Part of the how to come out at a job interview involves preparation. To prepare what you are going to say, you need to understand whom you are saying it to. That means conducting research on the company that you have applied to. It means finding out as much as you can about the people who could potentially be interviewing you for the position. Use all the resources you have available including the Internet, publications, social media, contacts, friends, family members, etc. Your goal is to get the job. The interview and the way

FACT

A recent study done by Harvard researcher Andras Tilcsik found that if you disclose the fact that you are a gay man on your resume, you are 60% more likely[20] to get an interview. They did, however, note that location plays a big role in the findings, with some areas being more progressive and inclusive than others.

---

20 "Why Gay Men Don't Get Job Interviews," The Week, http://theweek.com/article/index/220029/why-gay-men-dont-get-job-interviews

While being an LGBTQ employee should be a total non-issue at work, at this stage it can matter. Your circumstances and values will either guide you to come out at the interview or leave that information out completely. Either way, you will need to carry out research. Finding out what you should say during an interview is important if you want to nail it. It is like a double-edged sword. On one hand you are proud of who you are, and it should not be an issue. On the other hand, you have to accept that in business these ideals are not always met with enthusiasm.

You are the only one who knows your reasons for wanting to come out at the interview. If it makes you more comfortable to ensure that the company knows from the very beginning, then it is important that you create a strategy that will keep you looking like a great hire. That means knowing how to sell yourself. How does being an LGBTQ employee make you better at your job? Think about it, write it down and see if you can use any of your notes to articulate an answer.

How to Dress for an Interview

How does an LGBTQ job seeker dress for an interview? Much like everyone else does. You will have to find out what the acceptable dress code is and comply with it. Usually, business/professional attire is required.

Traditional career guides will segment tips in regards to dressing for an interview based on gender. Stern advice that men should always wear ties and women closed-toe pumps with a moderate to low heel is common. This resource calls for the discussion to move away from the stereotypical gender roles as it pertains to dress. There are several factors to identify:

⅄ *Know your audience:* Are you interviewing with a conservative organization, a more creative one, or a nonprofit organization?

⅄ *Know your comfort level:* Interviews can be stressful enough, adding an additional element of feeling uncomfortable can affect the entire process.

⅄ *Know yourself:* If a company is going to reject you at the interview stage based on what you were wearing, is that a company you want to work for?

Presenting as the gender you identify with is encouraged. The litmus test is asking yourself if what you are wearing is polished and professional. For those job seekers who are gender questioning or currently going through a gender transition, speaking to someone in the organization's human resources department may be an option and prevent any misunderstandings.

An example would include the historic ruling in 2012 in which the U.S. Equal Employment Opportunity Commission determined that job bias against employees on the basis of gender identity equates to sex discrimination under existing law. The determination came about as part of the resolution of a case involving Mia Macy, a transgender woman who allegedly was denied a job as a ballistics technician at the Bureau of Alcohol, Tobacco, Firearms and Explosives laboratory in Walnut Creek, California. While still presenting as male, Macy was told in January 2011 that she would receive a position she wanted at the Walnut Creek crime laboratory. As evidence of her impeding hire, Aspen of DC, the contractor responsible for filling the position, contacted her to begin the necessary paperwork and said an investigator was performing a background check. After informing the contractor that she would transition from male to female, Macy received an email from the contractor stating that the position, due to federal budget constraints, had been cut. Later, she was told someone else was awarded the position.

Regardless of sexual orientations and gender identities, there are several general rules that you should follow when dressing for a job interview:

- ▲ Stick to neutral colors that will not distract the interviewer from what you are saying. This is not the right time to wear that rainbow tie.
- ▲ Keep it simple; keep it formal.
- ▲ If the job allows for creativity, you can be a little more creative with your wardrobe.
- ▲ Do not do anything over-the-top, even if it is what you usually do.
- ▲ First impressions last. It should be based on what you SAY, not what you wear.
- ▲ Always err on the side of looking smart.
- ▲ If you can, see what other people wear at the organization and match it.
- ▲ Keep jewelry to a minimum; take out piercings in non-traditional, visible areas.

FACT

For some LGBTQ employees, dress codes can be an issue, because they may not conform to stereotypical styles. There are often crossovers in what is considered male or female clothing. In the workplace, you will need to know exactly what is okay to wear.

In an interview, you really want the interviewer to regard you as professional, well dressed, neat, and clean. If you can manage dressing in a way that will enhance these preferred characteristics, then you will be on your way to leaving a good impression.

Appropriate Behavior at Interviews

To be clear about this section, behavior is defined as actions, mannerisms, and reactions—including the way you speak, sit, walk—even your hand gestures.

Here are some excellent tips to keep you behaving like a winning applicant:

- Leave your emotions at the door. It does not matter if you have just broken up with your partner—an interview is not the time or the place to talk about personal or LGBTQ issues. Keep it strictly professional.

- Try to speak well; leave out any cursing; and be aware of your diction, verb tense, and pronunciation to make the conversation more formal. Remember, it is likely that you are not sitting across from one of your friends. In addition, if you do use the acronym LGBTQ, or any variation, be aware that the interview may ask you what it stands for.

- Sit down with your legs crossed or with your shoes flat on the ground in front of you. Keep your hands folded on your lap, until you speak—then you can use them to express your point.

- Part of your preparation strategy is to have preselected stories to share. These should illustrate different aspects about yourself and why you are the best candidate. If these stories include affiliations with queer activities, make sure that these stories really explain why you are a leader, or team player, problem solver or any other trait they are looking for in an employee.

⋏ From the very second you enter the building, everyone is your potential interviewer. Smile and be friendly to everyone! Never act bored or frustrated that they are running late. Being patient and kind are two traits every business looks for in employees.

⋏ When you first meet your interviewer, shake hands firmly. If your handshake style is a little weak, practice it before the interview. This common gesture often makes a big first impression.

⋏ Turn off your cell phone. A ringing phone from a briefcase or pocket during an interview can be detrimental. A vibrating phone can be distracting, as can a tone indicating a new text message, email, or status update notification. Also on the topic of cell phones, make sure that your outgoing voicemail message is clear and professional and no ring back tones. You want the employer to leave you a message that you got the job, not hang up out of concern or confusion.

It is most important to be confident and friendly at an interview. If you are a shy person, practice speaking with confidence. Always maintain eye contact with your interviewer; do not look down when you answer questions.

If you dress neatly and behave with respect, there is no reason why you should not make a good impression. The golden rule here is be yourself, and let them see what an asset you will be to the company. If you are not feeling comfortable about the interview process, practice with a friend or a professional at the local college or community center.

In summary, an interview is a conversation between you and the interviewer. The interviewer will determine if you are the best candidate for the position by evaluating the skills and abilities gained through your professional experiences, educational background, work experience, internships, volunteer experiences, class projects, course work, student group experience, and interests and hobbies. Just as with your resume, not discussing these because they connect you to the LGBTQ community could be selling yourself short and jeopardize your chances of being considered for the position.

It is important to understand that you are not only the interviewee, but also an interviewer. You will want to make sure that the position is one that aligns with your overall career goals. The interviewer will also assess if you will fit in at the organization. This will be determined if it is felt that you share the same values of the organization and if the interviewer can envision you working effectively with the team. You should also have a sense if the organization is right for you by the end of the interview.

4 Exercises on Successful Interviewing

1. At the interview, how would you disclose your gender identity or sexual orientation through your participation in an LGBTQ association?

_____

_____

_____

_____

_____

_____

_____

2. Lizzy is going to an interview at the corporate head offices of a fast food chain. She really wants to get this manager position to advance her career. But first she needs some advice on what to wear and how to behave. Can you give her some key points?

_____

_____

_____

_____

_____

_____

3. **Why is research an important step in the interview preparation process?**
   a. It allows you to create a game plan based on facts.
   b. It gives you an instant advantage over applicants that do not do research.
   c. It lets you know how to behave and dress.
   d. All of the above.

   A: d

4. **True or False. At the interview you can use LGBTQ affiliations to bolster academic or professional experiences.**

   A: True

CHAPTER 8

Coming Out
at Work

As for being out in Hollywood—I never thought about it. I never hid who I was."

JANE LYNCH
(LESBIAN, ACTOR)

Even if you have come out on your resume and in the interview, you will still have to contemplate how you are going to come out to colleagues—if that is what you decide to do. It is one thing to let the hiring manager know you are an LGBTQ candidate at the interview, and another to let the direct people you will be working with daily know as well.

This is a personal decision that you will have to make on your own, based on factors that will influence you when you are at work. For example, will you work closely with others as part of a team or will you have a more independent role? Will you have a supportive manager that you see often or a supervisor that gives a high level of autonomy? Is the nature of your work competitive or more collaborative? Will you be working in a space of your own or sharing space with colleagues? An environment where people are competing against each other can be very different than one where people are collaborating or depending on each other to do well. People working closely together in shared space are often more inclined to chat about their lives whereas being in your own office most of the day offers more privacy.

When to Come Out at Work

When is it a good idea to come out at work? On the very first day? After six months? After a year? While no one can make this decision for you, there are good reasons to come out at work sooner than later. For example, if you feel that it will make you more comfortable in the workplace to tell key people about your sexual orientation/gender identity then consider it. Also consider it if you think that it will be less of a distraction and allow you to focus on your daily tasks.

You do not have to walk in with a rainbow flag or bake a cake and announce it to the office! When you disclose it to key people in your immediate work life, chances are the information will get around to others. Being an LGBTQ employee may make you the center of office gossip for a while. That is when you need to show people that you are no different than they are. Do not let your LGBTQ status box you in and rob you of your other attributes. If you are an excellent copyeditor in a marketing firm, become known for it. You just change people's perceptions about what it means to be part of the queer community in the process.

ᒐ FACT

According to the General Social Survey[21] (GSS) 58% of LGB survey participants stated that they did not experience employment discrimination. Though data shows that levels of employment discrimination go up when LGB employees are open about their sexual orientation at work.

You might also want to let people know that you are LGBTQ if there is already talk about it in the office. If some people have assumed, then you may want to bring it up casually by mentioning something you did over the weekend with your

---

21 Steve Williams, "Report: It's Still Risky to Come Out at Work," http://www.care2. com/causes/report-its-still-risky-to-come-out-at-work.html

girlfriend or boyfriend. This will signal to them that you are open and confident.

How to Come Out at Work

There are a number of ways to come out at work, and none that seem easy when you are faced with the task! One factor to consider is how you will want to establish yourself as an employee before telling people about your sexual orientation/ gender identity. When you do this, you allow people to get to know you on a professional level first—before diving into the more personal information. This can make a big difference when you do finally come out in the workplace.

Use resources within the organization to assist you in this process. For example, you can use the company's intranet, the diversity or human resources department, or the queer employee resource group. These resources will be able to guide you through the process of coming out in a professional and acceptable manner.

 **SOMETHING TO THINK ABOUT**

If you feel that you want to disclose your sexual orientation to certain people in your workplace, then do so in a situation that makes you comfortable. If someone approaches you about it, use your best judgment.

It is imperative that you prepare yourself before you execute a coming out plan. Further, it is important to consider that once you have told some coworkers, you cannot take it back. The information will exist as public knowledge, even if you receive negative reactions from people in the office. Hopefully, you have chosen the company well and there will not be the slightest bit of negativity about your gender identity or sexual orientation. Until then, here are some points to consider when coming out at work:

- ⌃ Prepare yourself mentally for the process.
- ⌃ Choose whom you want to tell.
- ⌃ Decide where you are going to tell them.
- ⌃ Decide what you are going to say.
- ⌃ Decide how you are going to say it.

Keep the announcement brief and professional—this is, after all, information that is very personal to you, and while it is no one's business but yours, people may ask questions about it. That is why you need to be relaxed and honest about it, to put people at ease. Coming out at work is similar to coming out on your resume or during an interview. You need to plan for it, prepare for it —and carry it out with grace and professionalism. If you can do that, then disclosing such information may be less stressful.

Time, place, and method matter, of course, but no one can tell you exactly how to come out at work. Every situation is different, so you will need to consider the options and make a decision. Take time to think about it and write down a few notes.

Assessing the Office Vibe

A very important step is to assess the vibe in your office. Before coming out, you may want to see what people are like in the office and who might be offended or negative about your sexual orientation or gender identity when it comes up. If the environment in your office is creative and light-hearted, and a few other out queer employees work on your floor, then there is probably less reason to stress. This could be an indication that your office is clearly well integrated with diversity and you will not be considered a novelty.

If however, your office is extremely conservative and you cannot identify with anyone in the office who might also be an out LGBTQ person, you may consider treading lightly. This can be a much more hostile environment for you because the people have not had the opportunity to work with someone who is out and open beforehand. If you find you have an LGBTQ colleague who is not out at work, this may complicate matters for you as well.

Different offices have different levels of awareness that you will need to assess. Just by listening to conversations between people, you can gather whether or not they may be comfortable with you coming out or not. Most people are not monsters, and most of the time you may be able to come out and nobody will think twice about it. But be smart! If you are a professor in a very conservative university, in a state where there are no laws protecting your rights, you may consider otherwise.

FACT

Many LGBTQ people are afraid to come out at work because of what they perceive might happen to them. There is a real fear factor in the LGBTQ community that they will be overlooked for promotions, ostracized, or worse—which will harm their careers.

According to a study done by the Center for Work-Life Policy[22], 78% of closeted employees are likely to change jobs within three years. One reason for this may be the office environment and how difficult it is being around people who do not know who you are, whom you are with, or anything else about your life. Being comfortable and accepted at work is a key issue. Even heterosexual people strive for acceptance in office environments. Feel your way forward by checking out the office and the people. If you conclude that it is safe to proceed then do so. If you find that they are close-minded people who would not understand—then make a decision with that consideration.

Why You Should Come Out

In this day and age, the majority of companies do not want to be seen as discriminatory—which means that if you decide to come out and you do receive negative reactions, there are usually mechanisms within the organization to take this issue up within the company. Organizations can be respectfully accommodating when a real injustice has been committed. Support will always be available for you either at your company or with an LGBTQ community organization.

Coming out will free you from monitoring what you say or how you act and focus on the work and professional development. It can be horrible having to reign in your personality because the workplace demands it. Many people will argue that your sexual orientation and gender identity have nothing to do with your job. While this is strictly true, there is no doubt that it affects the way other people treat you—and THAT affects your job.

---

22 Brian McNaught, "Why Gays Should Come Out at Work," http://www.cnn.com/2011/OPINION/06/28/mcnaught.gays.workplace/index.html

Come out for the right reasons. Do so because you want to be accepted and you do not want to hide your true self. If you cannot be yourself at work, then it can be really hard to enjoy the experience. This is one reason why so many queer people change jobs so often—they continually search for better circumstances where they can be themselves and allow themselves the opportunity to truly love their jobs.

Sit down and write a few reasons why you want to come out at work. Read the paper a few days later. Do the reasons still seem valid? If they do, then you may have to plan how to tell individuals in the office. If not, hold onto the paper and make a note to look at it again at a later date. You can always go back to the list and edit it as you see necessary.

Many would argue that coming out at work is a must because you should be proud of who you are. Of course you should be proud and confident in yourself and in your abilities as an employee. However, you should not feel pressure to come out from anybody. If you choose to come out, you will do so when you feel comfortable. Everyone has his or her own reasons for coming out. Although it cannot be denied that there are benefits associated with being out and proud at the workplace, doing so before you are ready can be damaging personally and professionally.

Remember that your working environment is the one place where you will have to see the same people, daily—for a very long time if you want to build a career there. Your decisions affect these relationships, so if you do choose to come out, at least come out in a way that is respectful to your colleagues. Use this opportunity to form stronger bonds with the people in your team or department.

Weighing the Pros and Cons

To close this section, let us take a closer look at the pros and cons that you may encounter when deciding to come out at work.

The Pros

- ⅄ A lot of stress comes from hiding who you are. When you come out that stress is lifted to allow you to be the best at what you do.
- ⅄ You do not have to worry about switching pronouns when you talk about your significant other.
- ⅄ Being honest in the workplace means that you will make deeper, better relationships with the people who appreciate you just the way you are.
- ⅄ You will not have to lie about your life, what you did over the weekend or on vacation—and whom you did it with.
- ⅄ Just by being out and present you may be educating people how non-different queer professionals are. As a result people may be more respectful and not make wayward comments about LGBTQ people.
- ⅄ Your job productivity/performance is likely to improve because you will be in a totally comfortable environment.
- ⅄ You may serve as an example for other LGBTQ employees.

TIP

If you weigh the pros and cons— you may
see that it makes sense to come out at work,
especially if you have done your homework and
have chosen an LGBTQ–friendly workplace.

The Cons

- You may open yourself up to discrimination and prejudice in the workplace from colleagues and bosses.
- You may be treated differently when people find out that you are queer.
- People may not know how to treat your partner at work functions. You may experience some awkward moments.
- You might lose your job just because you decided to disclose your sexual orientation/gender identity.
- You may be overlooked for promotions or isolated because you are perceived as different from others in the office.

Weighing the pros and cons needs to be done by you, and no one else. You will have to live with these consequences, so it is important that you arrive at a decision that makes sense to you. If you are struggling to decide, speak to an association or your company's HR department—they may be able to provide guidance.

4 Exercises in Knowing When to Come Out

1. List three of your own reasons for wanting to come out in the workplace.

   a.

   b.

   c.

2. Jamie openly identifies as a lesbian and has recently started her first job as a financial analyst at one of New York's top firms. There is a work function coming up and she would like to take her partner. She's hesitant because her partner identifies as gender neutral. Her team has never made an issue about being a lesbian, however, she is not sure how they will react to her partner. What should Jamie do?

3. Identify the MAIN pro and the MAIN con when disclosing your sexual orientation or gender identity in the workplace?

   a. Comfort levels / being fired

   b. Honesty / discrimination

c. Being yourself/prejudice
d. Job performance/being treated differently
e. Acceptance/being overlooked

3.1. Write down why you feel that these are the most important pros and cons for you:

_____

_____

_____

_____

_____

4. When would you think twice about coming out at work?

_____

_____

_____

_____

_____

A: When your working environment may be hostile or conservative, when the company has no LGBTQ policy, when your state has no LGBTQ anti-discrimination laws.

5. True or False. If you identify as LGBTQ you must come out at work.
A: False

CHAPTER 9

Combating Discrimination Based on Sexual Orientation

"Each time we act against discrimination, we add a ring of life to the American tree of liberty."

JOHN BERRY
(GAY, GOVERNMENT OFFICIAL)

Congratulations! You conquered resume writing, aced the interview, got the job, and came out to colleagues and supervisors at work. You are being recognized for doing your job well, forming relationships with coworkers, and sharing your whole self at work. This euphoria however can be short lived in some cases. With such transparency, you may find yourself in the situation you feared most, being exposed to harassment or discrimination based on sexual orientation or gender identity. This sort of discrimination comes in many forms and can be challenging to prove. It is important you know how to deal with and combat discrimination in the workplace.

Defining Discrimination Based on Sexual Orientation and Gender Identity

There are many ways that someone can discriminate against you. However, the proper definition for sexual orientation and gender identity discrimination is as follows:

If you are treated differently in any way because of your sexual orientation/gender identity or perceived sexual orientation/gender identity—or because you associate with others of a perceived sexual orientation/gender identity—it could be considered direct discrimination. For example, your boss does not assign you to work on an account due to that fact that the client organization is known to be extremely conservative in nature. If a person at your company or the company itself imposes any sort of provision, practice, or criterion in action that puts you at a disadvantage to others, this could be considered indirect discrimination. For example, if the organization offers the benefit of free health club memberships to husbands and wives of employees, but does not extend the same benefit to same sex couples.

Similarly, if you are subjected to some sort of detriment because of an action your company, or someone in your company has performed an action that conflicts with the internal equality policy—this could be considered victimization. If you experience unwanted conduct related to sexual orientation that violates your personal dignity and creates a hostile, degrading, intimidating, offensive, or humiliating environment—this can be considered harassment.

 SOMETHING TO THINK ABOUT

No matter the term used to describe the mistreatment you may experience, it is important to let key people within the organization know what is happening. HR professionals will often step in and ensure that it does not happen again. All too often, LGBTQ employees simply leave the workplace, instead of reporting the discrimination and standing up for their basic human rights.

Examples of Discrimination

- ⋏ Not being hired because you are an LGBTQ candidate.
- ⋏ Not having the same access to promotions or incentives as others.
- ⋏ Being transferred because you are an LGBTQ person.
- ⋏ Not being trained properly because you are a queer employee.
- ⋏ Being treated badly or visibly differently because you are LGBTQ.
- ⋏ Not being taken seriously because of your sexual orientation or gender identity.

What to Do if You Face Discrimination

As an employee, what can you do if you are faced with the sad reality of discrimination in the workplace? The very first thing you should do is try to identify what sort of discrimination you have encountered so that you can better explain it to a manager, human resources staff member, or lawyer. It is best to take some notes right after the incident while it is fresh in your mind including exact quotes, the time and date of the incident, the name of anyone who witnessed it, how you reacted, and other details.

Once you have identified what sort of discrimination you are up against, detail whether it is an isolated incident or an on-going problem. Find out if any of your colleagues experienced the discrimination alongside you. If yes, take them with you to see the HR manager or your department boss.

> ## 🔍 FACT
>
> Many companies have their own policies for dealing with all forms of discrimination in the workplace. These policies will help protect you if something has happened that you need to report. Stick to the facts; all parties will be questioned and held accountable for what transpired.

It is always a good idea to try and resolve discrimination issues internally. Managers should be willing to listen to your concerns—it is their job to sort out this kind of problem. Report what happened and ask if the manager can ensure it will not happen again. If it is a manager who is discriminating against you, you will need to find a more senior person to talk to—perhaps the general manager or even the HR director of the company. They will likely appreciate that you brought the issues to light.

If the issue cannot be resolved internally, then legal action may be an option. Depending on the situation and the state you live in, you may have a case against the individual, the company, or both. You may want to start by contacting a local LGBTQ rights association, national organization such as ACLU, or a lawyer. Representatives will be able to provide you next steps in the process. One consideration is that taking action may draw attention to you and the subject matter. Will you be okay with that kind of spotlight and any issues that spring from it? It is something to think about.

Forms of Discrimination

Discrimination can rear its ugly head in many ways, but it can also feel like it is nearly impossible to prove. A slur about queer people said in jest may not have been intentionally hurtful, but you can find yourself in emotional distress about it none-the-less. That is why you should understand the various forms of discrimination. When you can identify what has happened, you are better equipped to deal with it.

- ▲ *Intentional or negligent infliction of emotional distress:* When someone is called a fag in the office, this can result in emotional distress. It could be considered a form of sexual orientation discrimination.

- ▲ *Assault:* Assault occurs when a person makes threats of force or attempts to cause injury to another person. If this occurs because of your sexual orientation/gender identity it can be discrimination. It is also illegal to assault a person in any context and can be subject to criminal charges.

- ▲ *Battery:* Battery is when a person actually causes injury to another. Battery involves any sort of illegal touching that is unwanted and perpetrated by an aggressor. For example, if you are shoved harshly because of your sexual orientation or gender identity. Again, such action can be subject to criminal charges.

- ▲ *Harassment:* Harassment occurs when someone continually engages in unwanted action towards you because of your sexual orientation or gender identity. For example, every time you step away from your cubical somebody leaves a note with homophobic sentiment.

TIP

If you are not sure who is discriminating against you, but it is clearly happening—you need to contact your manager immediately. Nipping small instances in the bud is important if you are going to continue a healthy, happy work experience.

▲ *Invasion of privacy:* If someone is invading your privacy because of your sexual orientation/gender identity, then it is clear-cut discrimination. Looking through your phone, email, coming to your house uninvited – these are just some forms considered invasions of privacy.

▲ *Defamation:* If there is an individual in the workplace who does not like you because of your sexual orientation/ gender identity, it can be very difficult to thrive in that environment. They may say things about you to others or make up stories to put you in a bad light.

▲ *Employment interference or wrongful termination:* If someone tries to get you fired by hindering your job performance or sabotaging you—that is discrimination. If you are fired because you are an LGBTQ employee, and for no other reason, then it is considered wrongful termination in some states.

Examples of Workplace Discrimination

It is critical that you get a firm grasp of what constitutes discrimination. Here are some examples based on actual cases of discrimination in action in the workplace.

⅄ A finance manager started a new job and was fired just three months later. He felt he was constantly disciplined and harassed more vigorously than his peers. He believed that the harassment was linked to his sexual orientation, because the adverse treatment began shortly after he came out to his boss. The company eventually settled and compensated the employee for the harassment and wrongful termination.

⅄ A pharmaceutical representative that was required to travel to 12 locations each month was referred to as a 'the dyke' at a few of the locations. She was also ridiculed in front of customers when she made deliveries. One location in particular was unbearable. Eventually, she reported the discrimination to the head office, and all 12 locations were made to attend workshops on discrimination in the workplace.

⅄ A branch manager of a retail store was removed from a project involving children because he began transitioning from male to female. The other managers and CEO said that there were other reasons for removing the manager from the project, but the branch manager did not believe them. Eventually, the situation was resolved and the manager took part in the proposed project.

⅄ A PR consultant believed that she was constantly being harassed by her supervisor and colleagues because she came out as bisexual and openly discussed having dates with both males and females. Along with being called names, she was excluded from projects. She filed a complaint against one of the men in her office that would not leave her alone. She decided to move companies, but was compensated for her distress.

TIP

If you are an LGBTQ job seeker, it can be harder for some people to accept you simply because they have not had the opportunity to work with someone like you. If coworkers ask because they are interested, use it as an opportunity to educate them about the LGBTQ community.

These examples give you a fairly good idea of discrimination that can exist in the workplace. Of course, you can never tell if it is going to happen, why, or when—that depends on the people involved. Just be aware that even at the most LGBTQ-friendly companies, homophobic people could still exist.

Important Job Rights to Know

There are a few job rights that you need to be aware of so that you are equipped with the best information in the event that something does happen. Keep in mind that choosing an LGBTQ-friendly company can better prevent these things from occurring, therefore minimizing the chances of becoming a victim of discrimination.

⌅ The Don't Ask Don't Tell law was repealed recently, which means that gay and lesbian military personnel are now free to join the military and serve the country openly. The repeal means that you are no longer required by law to keep your sexual orientation a secret if you are a member of the military.

▲ State laws offering protection such as those in Alaska, California, and Hawaii generally prohibit sexual orientation discrimination in the workplace. You will need to look into which states have these laws, and if they apply to your situation.

▲ Transgender employees have rights based on law in certain states that cover gender identity discrimination. In these states, you have the legal right to exist in the workplace free of discrimination.

As an employee, you have the moral right to NOT be discriminated against at work. That is really the core of it. While there are not many laws that cover queer people completely, it once again speaks to how important choosing the right company can be. If you choose an organization with a great anti-discrimination policy, then you are more likely to be covered at work should anything happen. The companies that promote diversity have a number of processes that spring into action when discrimination does occur. They are very well versed in swiftly dealing with the matter and correcting it. If the problems persist, do not be afraid to speak out about it and do not feel like you are alone. There are LGBTQ advocacy organizations and associations that can help you.

3 Exercises in Identifying Discrimination

1. *Name five different types of LGBTQ employee discrimination.*

   a.

   b.

   c.

   d.

   e.

   A: indirect discrimination, direct discrimination, harassment, defamation, battery, assault, invasion of privacy, emotional distress.

2. *Alex worked happily as a tech supervisor for an app development company for three years and just recently started a gender transition from female to male. A new manager started and suddenly the dynamic in the office changed. Alex was being excluded from meetings, was not receiving emails or briefs, and on several occasions heard the new boss refer to him as that 'cross dresser.' Alex had expected a promotion that year, but it was given to someone who was actually his junior. What kind of discrimination is Alex experiencing and how should he handle it?*

3. Where should you report that you have been discriminated
    against based on sexual orientation/gender identity?
    a. The police department
    b. Your superiors at work
    c. An LGBTQ employee resource group
    d. The human resources department
    e. Your work colleagues
    f. b, c, d
    g. All of the above

    A: f

CHAPTER 10

Using Social Media to Find a Job

"Hopefully people can look at me and realize that it's okay to be open in their lives and be themselves and do great work and make contributions to the world as scientist."

CAROLYN BERTOZZI
(LESBIAN, SCIENTIST)

Social media is not a new concept, but what is new is just how powerful of a tool it has become for job seekers. People are finding jobs via sites such as LinkedIn, Facebook, Twitter, Biznik, and Entrepreneur Connect every day. You need to learn how to harness the power of social media to complement your job search strategy.

The Use of Social Media by Employers and LGBTQ Job Seekers

Social media is not just a fun way to pass the time anymore. Increasingly companies are using a person's social profile as a way to learn more about candidates before the interview process. As well as having a professional social profile, you need to tap into the thousands of jobs being shared on Facebook pages, in LinkedIn groups, and on Twitter. Social media really can be your secret job finding weapon.

Using social media allows you to connect with the pages of individuals and groups that are part of local LGBTQ community. These pages often post jobs that are of interest to their LGBTQ fans or members. The bottom line here is that your potential employers are using social media, you use social media—and so does everyone else. It is a fast and efficient way to find jobs, not to mention a simple way to find LGBTQ-friendly work environments.

⟨ FACT

Did you know that 64% of all companies in the US use two or more social media channels? According to Jobvite[23], 43% of their employee social referral hires come from Facebook, and 73% of social hires come from LinkedIn.

When your social networks consist of LGBTQ individuals/communities, LGBTQ friendly companies, professional connections, and friends—it will not be long before you hear of a job that suits you. These jobs are always floating around, and more importantly—they may not be posted anywhere else.

If you need another reason why, here is one: your LGBTQ competitor applicants are using social media to grab all the best jobs from you. These days you are either using social media to advance your career, or others are using it to leave you in their dust!

How to Use Search Engine Filters

A search engine is a very large program that is used to retrieve data, files, or documents from a database or network. The most common search engine in the world is Google, but you could also use MSN, Yahoo, or Bing. People generally know how to use search engines, but for a queer person it would certainly help if you knew the finer details of advanced search and filtering information. That way, you can find the best pages whenever you are looking for something specific within a local area or within the LGBTQ community.

---

23 The State of Social Recruiting in 2011 Infographic, http://thenickyblog.com/2011/08/people-jobs-social-media-infographic.html

---

⌕ FACT

A very small number of people bother to use the appropriate search operators to refine their searches on Google and on other search sites. This means their searches are not as detailed or streamlined as could be.

Using the search bar is not as simple as typing in the keywords. There are other commands that you can use to get more accurate answers. Note that you may want to try alternative forms of the acronym LGBTQ such as LGBT and GLBT to improve results. Here are a few tips to consider:

- Exact word or phrase search can be conducted on Google by using quotation marks to identify the phrase. Example: "LGBT association in Maryland"
- Want to get to an organization's job page quickly? Try including the phrase "jobsite:" plus the name of the company. For example, if you want to check out jobs at Marriott Hotel it would look like this: jobsite:marriott.com
- Use the tilde sign (~) to include synonyms in order to increase search results. For example: ~queer professionals. Results will include terms queer, gay, lesbian, etc.

Which Platforms Are Most Useful?

There are some excellent social media platforms that you can use to find LGBTQ friendly employers. The trick is to find LGBTQ recruitment groups, pages, or companies within these social media sites, and join their social community.

⅄ **LinkedIn:** By far the best business professional site on the Internet, LinkedIn has thousands of LGBTQ groups and agencies that would welcome you into their networks. If you do not have a LinkedIn account yet, sign up for one now. After doing so you will need to complete your profile, post a professional photo, and add contacts. Next, use the search bar in LinkedIn to connect with LGBTQ individuals and groups, individuals and groups within your industry, and those individuals and groups in your geographic area. Now it is time to join the discussions! Post discussions, comment on posts from others, and show that you are someone to be noticed professionally. LinkedIn also has job listings. Choose the jobs tab and enter a job title, keywords, or a company name to get your job search started.

⅄ **Facebook:** The world's largest and most popular social network once again swoops in as one of the most useful platforms for job seekers. Before using your Facebook page for your job search, make sure that your privacy settings are set correctly and do not use an inappropriate profile picture or cover photo.

⅄ How can you use Facebook as a part of your job search? The first is the most obvious, networking! Did you meet a recruiter of a company that you would like to work for at a career fair? Search for the individual and check to see if you have common friends or even consider sending a friend request. You can also update your employment history under the about section or post a status update announcing what type of work you are looking for. Ask your friends to share the update with their friends to cast a wider net. In addition, consider joining and actively participating in Facebook groups.

Denver's Gay Professionals is a group that you might want to join. It states that the mission of the group is to provide a space where individuals are encouraged to network. Finally, why not create and post an ad? A short bio and a link to your online resume can create a buzz. Unlike other advertising, you can get started with a Facebook ad for just a dollar a day.

A **Twitter:** Again, as in the case of your Facebook page, it is suggested that before you use your Twitter account as a part of your job search strategy, ensure it does not contain any content that might have an employer second-guessing.

A Now that your Twitter account is employer friendly, click on the #Discover tab and then the browse categories tab. You can enter the word jobs into the search box. Scroll down results to find organizations and positions you find interesting. Do not see the job you are looking for today? Elect to follow the organization so that you can receive updates. Next try using hashtags. Examples include #jobs, #techjobs, and #recruiting. Finally, do not underestimate the power of following individuals who are industry leaders and tweeting sharp and relevant responses that demonstrate your knowledge and passion for your vocation.

 TIP

Find the platforms that you enjoy using the most. You will only make the most of these platforms if you are using them regularly. Do not for example, sign up to LinkedIn, join groups—and then do nothing.

- **Biznik:** Biznik is a business-networking site for independent businesses, freelancers, and business owners. It is a good place to establish a name for yourself, and to make great contacts with business owners in your field. Who knows, instead of starting your first job, you could be starting your own company. It is all about finding the right people and collaborating with them for mutual benefit.

- **Myspace:** If you are in a creative field, then Myspace is the place to be. Music, video, and media attract all sorts of big companies, and you can connect with some very important people here. It is also great if you have a portfolio and can upload it to Myspace as part of your resume when you apply for jobs.

If there are any other social networking sites that you believe will help you find your perfect job, then by all means join them. Google+ and Pinterest are two other options, though they do have limited use, and can take your time away from the sites that will get you more results as an LGBTQ job seeker.

Your Mini Social Media Strategy

Using social media to find jobs is just one piece of the puzzle. Companies also use social media to check out if you are qualified enough to be invited for an interview. These days, your social profile and what the Internet says about you can definitely be the difference between landing a good job and a great one. That is why you need a mini job sourcing strategy. Follow these steps and you will be getting interviews in no time:

Step #1: Search yourself.

Find out what your social profile looks like from the outside.

The truth is that although you may not be planning to come out at work, individuals may already know that you are part of the LGBTQ community based on your social profile. If you do not want people to know or if there are unprofessional photos or videos of you online—get rid of them!

Step #2: Redo all of your images and text.

Clean up your social profile by adding clean-cut images and respectable, career-orientated text to descriptions. This is most important on sites such as LinkedIn, where people associate the site with a high level of professionalism.

Step #3: Outline which platforms you will be using.

A strategy is something you can use repeatedly and that works over time. To make it work, you need to identify which platforms will be best for you. It is pretty easy to decide, just ask yourself, "Where are the job opportunities?"

📝 TIP

Set aside some time each day to visit your chosen platforms and do the work that is required there. Job seeking is about searching, filtering, locating, and applying. This process takes time and not all resumes you send in will get a favorable response.

Step #4: Outline when you will respond and how.

When you begin to receive job posts, you may need to set aside some time each day to review them—and to conduct LGBTQ research. Then you may need to outline HOW you will respond to each job posting. This needs to be done professionally, or not at all. Do not rush!

Step #5: Be active on the social networking pages.

Contribute, like, share, comment, and make friends with the communities that are involved with your job seeking process. Sometimes you can get additional benefits from being engaging on social media pages. Plus, it is part of your networking strategy to meet new people.

If you follow these five basic steps, you will find that using social media to source jobs is an excellent way to spend your time. You may be amazed at the gems you can find on social media outlets that are not posted anywhere else. It is a simple fact companies just now prefer using social media to find applicants.

Finding an LGBTQ Friendly Workplace with Social Media

Social media is a wonderful resource for queer job seekers. Here is how you should find LGBTQ friendly workplaces using the social media platforms that have been outlined.

➤ On Facebook use the search bar to locate and like the LGBTQ associations related to your profession or interests. For example, if you type in 'LGBTQ nurses', you will be directed to the Nurses PUSH (Penn Understanding Sexuality in Healthcare) page. The mission of the group includes assisting members of the LGBTQ community to achieve their full potential in nursing. There you can comment on posts, share information, find out about open lectures and networking opportunities, and upcoming recruiting events.

⅄ Use the lists that are recommended in this book to connect with specific organizations on their social media pages. If you want to work for Lockheed Martin, for example, then simply search for their respective social media pages and connect. You will find that companies such as Lockheed Martin often updates their social pages with details about job openings in specific areas. Plus, you may get to virtually meet employees from Lockheed Martin, and get the ball rolling on becoming one yourself!

⅄ On LinkedIn you can connect with LGBTQ organizations, groups, and individuals. Actively participate in the discussions. You will begin to see the job opportunities arise—either in the form of posts or just as a result of putting the word out that you are looking for a position in a particular field.

⅄ Join the pages of all the LGBTQ-friendly employers that you want to keep an eye on. While these companies may not have the job you want now, you never know when your opportunity is going to present itself.

⅄ Create a few Google bookmarks/alerts for specific terms using your newfound search filter skills. Include your area and an organization that you want to watch. When any news, articles, job posts, or general information about the company that hits on these keywords, you will be notified.

If you stick to your mini social media strategy, you will see how effective social media can be at getting you closer to your ideal job. Too often, job seekers only use outdated methods of trying to find work—such as browsing through job sites and checking out directories and newspapers.

4 Exercises in Using Social Media for Job Searches

1. *How can social media bring you closer to your goal of finding that ideal LGBTQ-friendly job?*

_____

_____

_____

_____

2. *Dale is a career-driven job seeker who identifies as gay. He struggles to find great jobs online because of his poor search skills. In fact, Dale does not even know that there are different ways to search for information. Can you list at least four ways that you can use search filters to narrow down your search results?*

   a)

   b)

   c)

   d)

3. *Which platforms would you prefer spending time on and using for job seeking purposes? Rate them from 1-5 (1=lowest preference 5=highest preference)*

   a. Face book

   b. LinkedIn

   c. Twitter

   d. Biznik

  e. Myspace

  f. Google+ and Pinterest

3.1 *Briefly outline a quick one-hour strategy that involves your top three social platforms. Indicate what you are going to do on them and for how long each day.*

  1.

  2.

  3.

4. *List five organizations that are LGBTQ-friendly and that you would like to work for one day.*

  1.

  2.

  3.

  4.

  5.

CHAPTER 11

Career Search
Networking

They always say time changes things, but you actually have to change them yourself."

ANDY WARHOL
(GAY, ARTIST)

In order to be successful these days and to find the ideal position at a company that respects LGBTQ employees—you have to be a voracious networker. Networking is about establishing relationships with people that you meet, purely for career purposes. Networking can happen in person, electronically, or a combination of both these days. However you decide to expand your network know this—it will be one of the most valuable assets that you create for yourself in your chosen field.

How to Network for an Increase in Job Potential

There are many resources available to you online that will help you kick start becoming a part of certain exclusive networks that will improve your hiring potential. With social media these days, there are literally hundreds of ways you can become a professional networker.

Why would you want to become a great networker?

- To become part of a community that makes it easier for you to find LGBTQ-friendly employers.
- Build relationships with the right people to improve your career.
- Get better connected by knowing more people.

- ▲ Receive the career help you are looking for from LGBTQ professionals.
- ▲ Gain access to mentors in your industry that can help you improve your career.

All of these reasons and more should be the driving force behind your continued networking ambition. Take advantage of the available tools and resources that exist for you:

- ▲ LGBTQ associations and organizations
- ▲ LGBTQ student campus groups
- ▲ Online LGBTQ recruitment networks
- ▲ Special LGBTQ job sites and groups

📝 TIP

You can join any number of LGBTQ networking organizations online that will connect you to professionals and business owners. This is how you can get invited to professional networking events and functions. This is where you may meet some great people in your area of career interest.

Networking will take your career search to new heights, so it is something you really want to focus on. You can achieve more in less time—if you meet the right people in your field. Plus, you can count on support from these networks if you are ever exposed to discrimination in the workplace.

LGBTQ Campus Groups and Community Associations

For college students that identify as queer, it is important that you build quality relationships with your campus LGBTQ group. The members of such groups are likely to be the next generation of employees, supervisors, and presidents of organizations. They may be the people who are going to give you a great boost in your career down the road. For those individuals already in the workforce, it is as equally important that you build quality relationships with LGBTQ community associations. These associations are packed with other LGBTQ professionals that can lend support, advice, and even knowledge of job opportunities.

Every LGBTQ campus group or community association has a specific mission. You may want to review the group's mission statement before joining or participating in any activities. Most groups and associations, however, share a common vision:

- To provide support for their LGBTQ members' interests.
- To promote LGBTQ community service to their members.

- To make others aware of the issues that LGBTQ individuals face on a daily basis.
- To provide resources to its LGBTQ members, so they are better equipped to find good information and make more informed choices.
- Finally, to serve as a support mechanism for LGBTQ members entering the job market.

SOMETHING TO THINK ABOUT

Joining an LGBTQ campus group or community association will allow you the opportunity to build relationships with individuals preparing to transition from academia to the workplace or those already in the workforce. These relationships could prove beneficial when looking for a job in the future.

How to Form Relationships with Groups and Associations

If you have been on the outside of these campus groups and community associations for most of your life, and have never really wanted to become actively involved in the LGBTQ community for whatever reason—you may find yourself struggling to form these relationships. There can be a reluctance to get involved with LGBTQ associations, especially if you are not really an organization type of person. However, consider that making any effort could greatly benefit you.

Here are five proven ways you can form better relationships with your LGBTQ campus group/ community association.

1. Attend an LGBTQ campus group or community association meeting.
2. Go to an LGBTQ-specific event that is organized by your campus group or community association.

3. Once you have gotten to know some people, offer to help with meetings or to lend a hand organizing for the next event.

4. Connect with your LGBTQ campus group or community association members on Facebook and other social media channels.

5. Keep in touch with members even after you have graduate or move.

Conferences, Career Fairs, and Recruiting Events

Something you must consider doing is attending a variety of LGBTQ specific conferences, career fairs, or recruitment events. The networking that you can do at these events is really something you will not find anywhere else. OUT for Work (www.outforwork.org) hosts an annual industry inclusive career conference that addresses the specific needs of LGBTQ college students transitioning from academia to the workplace. The program is packed with speakers, breakout sessions, and networking opportunities. A career fair with organizations that support LGBTQ inclusion concludes the two-day conference.

A wide range of people that could make a real impact on your career attends LGBTQ specific events. For example, career fairs are frequented by specific organizations and businesses that actively seek out LGBTQ employees to improve their workplace diversity. Conferences may be an opportunity for you to speak to a queer employee and receive insight on what it is really like to be out and open in the workplace. Further, these individuals are likely to have networks of their own and willing to make an introduction on your behalf.

LGBTQ recruiting events are a superb place to find good, reputable people who may be able to help in your job search. All you have to do is attend these events and network. Bring along a few well-placed questions and a friendly-attitude, and you could be hooked up with an interview at a top organization, with a recommendation from one of their employees.

Networking cannot be understated, especially because you are an LGBTQ person. You may face many challenges in your career, so it is a good idea to have a network of support behind you. When you do, you will find that you are able to excel in your career. Schedule it in your calendar—attend an LGBTQ event.

Other Networking Opportunities

There are lots of other networking opportunities that may not necessarily be LGBTQ specific, but are equally as important to finding a good job.

- ▲ Join a few LinkedIn LGBTQ professional networks, where you will be able to meet and chat to people in your field. The LGBT Network Leadership & Pride is the largest group in the world for this, with more than 16,000 members. Some of these LGBTQ people are very influential, and may become great people to know for the future.

- ▲ Find LGBTQ recruitment networks online. There you can login, upload your resume, and receive updates on all the latest applicable jobs going for you in your area of focus. These are especially great for mid-level to senior executives or employees that have more than five years of experience.

⅄ Join Out & Equal's LGBTCareerLink. You will have access to numerous resources and can browse through jobs from LGBTQ-friendly companies. Connect with the group via LinkedIn and start networking with other LGBTQ professionals and allies.

⌕ FACT

The more active you are with networking, the wider you cast your net. That means when you look for a job you will have more options, job opportunities, and contacts. Then you can make an educated decision about the jobs you want to apply for, so that you end up somewhere comfortable and inclusive.

Keep your eyes open for any additional networking opportunities that arise. Being a member of LGBTQ career sites means that you can be alerted every time they host a recruiting or networking event. You may be able to attend LGBTQ friendly seminars, conferences, workshops, and expos, all because you took the time to put yourself on their email list.

Additional networking opportunities also arrive from the individuals you meet at these events. You may be invited to a specific work event or even a social occasion that could lead to advancement in your career. You have to be as ambitious as you can be, and use your relationships to make your way to the top. Expand your network weekly, and soon your career will take off.

4 Exercises in Career Search Networking

1. *Why is it important to focus on growing your network of LGBTQ contacts?*

2. *Dakota, who identifies as a pansexual, recently graduated with a degree in psychology. She really wants to find a great first job, but knows absolutely no one in the field. What advice would you give her?*

3. *Name five ways you can network and gain valuable LGBTQ contacts in your career.*

   1.

   2.

   3.

   4.

   5.

   A: Social media, joining LGBTQ recruitment sites, getting involved in your LGBTQ campus groups and associations, attending LGBTQ career events, being recruited by a company at a queer career fair.

4. *Name four goals of an LGBTQ campus or community group and then explain how these goals can help you advance in your career.*

   a. Support, advice, understanding, resources

   b. Advice, friendship, career, education

   c. Resources, tools, guide, plan

   d. Understanding, education, fun, parties

   A: All the above. Which are most important to you? Why?

   _____

   _____

   _____

   _____

Conclusion

It is important to allow people who want to be positive contributors of our society regardless of sex, race, creed and gender to reach their human potential."

GEORGINA BEYER
(TRANSGENDER, MEMBER OF NEW ZEALAND'S NATIONAL LEGISLATURE)

You are a proud, independent LGBTQ person with an outstanding career ahead of you. Now that you have the tools you need to survive and thrive in the workplace—there is nothing to stop you!

In our careers, we will be faced with hardships, obstacles, and difficulties that we will have to overcome. As long as you still have that fire to be the best and to do your best, there are plenty of awesome people in this world that will help you, if you need it.

Learn to be strong for yourself in your career. Stand up for what is right and fair, and never accept anything less than what you are worth. There are always multiple paths ahead of us, and when things occur that slow our pace or lead us down strange side roads— we can stop, reassess and take action, or continue in the wrong direction.

Your sexual orientation and gender identity may affect how people treat you in the workplace, but if you are true to yourself, you work hard and you smash through the discrimination and prejudicial opinions of a few people, you can and will have an amazing career. Opportunities are not given to those individuals that wait idly around—you have to find them!

Use the tools and advice in this book to move forward with your chosen career. Never let anyone or anything stand in your way. You need to have the kind of conviction that will carry you ahead of others in your career, even though you are made to face challenges.

Let these challenges build character in you, so you can grow and become better at your job. You ideal career is waiting for you; all you have to do is reach out and take it. To do that effectively means you might ask for help one day, and now you know how to get it.

Know your rights. Know that you are entitled to be everything you can be. Find a mentor. Make mistakes. Join associations. Make friends. Do extraordinary things in your career.

Your future will always be as bright as you intend it to be.

To your queer career,

Riley B. Folds

Useful LGBTQ Resources

Here are some excellent resources that I have compiled. I hope that they make your LGBTQ job search and experience a lot easier. Please note that this list is not exclusive and some information may have changed since this book was written.

National Resources

American Civil Liberties Union – Lesbian Gay & Transgender Project
125 Broad Street, 18th Floor
New York, NY 10004
Tel: 212-549-2627
Website: www.aclu.org/lgbt-rights

The mission of the project is the creation of a society in which lesbian, gay, bisexual and transgender (LGBT) people enjoy the constitutional rights of equality, privacy and personal autonomy, and freedom of expression and association.

CenterLink LGBT Community Center Member Directory
P.O. Box 24490
Fort Lauderdale, FL 33307
Tel: 954-765-6024
Email: CenterLink@lgbtcenters.org
Website: www.lgbtcenters.org/Centers/find-a-center.aspx

This association works to improve or enhance the existence of LGBTQ community centers. There are many networking opportunities available if you contact them. In addition, they have access to a nationwide directory of centers.

Gay & Lesbian Advocates & Defenders (GLAD)
30 Winter Street, Suite 800
Boston, MA 02108
Tel: 617-426-1350
Email: gladlaw@glad.org
Website: www.glad.org

GLAD is a very well-known legal rights organization based in New England. Programs are dedicated to ending discrimination based on sexual orientation, HIV status and gender identity and expression.

Gay and Lesbian National Hotline
2261 Market Street
San Francisco, CA 94114
Tel: 888-THE-GLNH (888-843-4564)
Email: info@GLBTNationalHelpCenter.org
Website: www.glnh.org

GLNH is a nonprofit organization that provides free counseling and support to LGBTQ people that are going through tough times.

Lambda Legal National Headquarters
120 Wall Street, Suite 1500
New York, NY 10005
Tel: 212-809-8585
Website: www.lambdalegal.org

Lambda Legal is a national organization committed to achieving full recognition of the civil rights of lesbians, gay men, bisexuals, transgender people and those with HIV through impact litigation, education and public policy work.

National Center for Lesbian Rights National Office
870 Market Street, Suite 370
San Francisco, CA 94102
Tel: 415-392-6257
Website: www.nclrights.org

The National Center for Lesbian Rights is a national legal organization committed to advancing the civil and human rights of lesbian, gay, bisexual, and transgender people and their families through litigation, public policy advocacy, and public education.

OUT for Work
1325 Massachusetts Ave. NW,
7th Floor, Suite 700, #702
Washington, DC 20005
Tel: 866-571-LGBT
Email: info@outforwork.com
Website: www.outforwork.org

OUT for Work is a nonprofit organization that serves as a complimentary component in the total educational experience of LGBTQ students, primarily in the development, evaluation, initiation and implementation of career plans and opportunities.

Pride at Work/AFL-CIO National Headquarters
815 16th Street NW
Washington, DC 20006
Tel: 202-637-5085
Email: info@prideatwork.org
Website: www.prideatwork.org

Pride at Work is a constituency group of the American Federation of Labor and Congress of Industrial Organizations. They work to unite the LGBTQ community with the labor movement, to rally around economic and social justice for the people.

The Legal Aid Society–Employment Law Center (Administrative headquarters)
180 Montgomery Street, Suite 600
San Francisco, CA 94104
Tel: 415-864-8848
Website: www.las-elc.org

LAS ELC focuses on a wide range of legal issues, but also handles LGBTQ cases. They host workshops and provide support and assistance for people in tough spots in the workplace.

The Pipeline Project – Careers in the LGBT Movement
C/o Astraea Lesbian Foundation for Justice
116 East 16th Street, 7th Floor
New York, NY 10003
Email: jobs@lgbtpipeline.org
Website: www.lgbtpipeline.org/lgbt-movement-careers

Whether you're a student looking for an internship or first-time job or a professional looking for a mid-career shift, the Pipeline Project can connect you with exciting opportunities in the LGBT Movement.

Resources Specific to Transgender Individuals

Center for Gender Sanity
PO Box 30313
Bellingham, WA 98228
Tel: 360-398-2878
Email: director@gendersanity.com
Website: www.gendersanity.com

The Center for Gender Sanity has a great program that helps transgender people transition if they are currently employed. It is called 'transitions that work' and it educates people in a corporate environment about transsexuals and helps them deal with the transition of their co-worker.

National Center for Transgender Equality
1325 Massachusetts Avenue, Suite 700
Washington, DC 20005
Tel: 202-903-0112
Email: NCTE@NCTEquality.org
Website: www.transequality.org

The National Center for Transgender Equality (NCTE) is a 501(c)3 social justice organization dedicated to advancing the equality of transgender people through advocacy, collaboration and empowerment.

Sylvia Rivera Law Project
147 W 24th St, 5th Floor
New York, NY 10011
Tel: 212-337-8550
Email: info@srlp.org
Website: www.srlp.org

This organization makes sure that everyone is free to express their gender identity in any way they see fit. They work against transgender discrimination, violence and harassment and try to improve equality for transgender individuals in the US.

Transgender at Work
Email: mah@mhorton.net
Website: www.tgender.net/taw

This project provides educational resources to employers that want to educate their employees about transgender employees. This is aimed at putting the transgender person at ease, so that they can be happy and productive.

Transgender Law Center
870 Market Street, Suite 400
San Francisco, CA 94102
Tel: 415-865-0176
Email: info@transgenderlawcenter.org
Website: www.transgenderlawcenter.org

TLC is a nonprofit organization that takes on transgender legal battles. This nonprofit has many experts and lawyers so that they can achieve their organizational goal of enhancing transgender equality in the US.

Transgender Law and Policy Institute
Email: query@transgenderlaw.org
Website: www.transgenderlaw.org

TLPI is a nonprofit that aims to help transgender individuals by watching policy developments and legal issues on the subject. They work on behalf of transgender clients as well, who have been discriminated against in the workplace.

Education and Information about the Workplace

Common Ground
Tel: 303-941-2991
Email: LWinfeld@common-grnd.com
Website: www.common-grnd.com

Common Ground is an education-based firm that does consulting work centered on workplace diversity. There are many sexual orientation programs to choose from, and they also work on employment policy for businesses.

Human Rights Campaign
1640 Rhode Island Ave. N.W.
Washington, DC 20036-3278
Tel: 202-628-4160
Toll free: 800-777-4723
Website: www.hrc.org

Humans Rights Campaign is easily the largest and most well-known civil rights organization in the LGBTQ community. They work tirelessly to improve equality and to prevent LGBTQ discrimination in the workplace, and in other areas. With more than 1.5 million members it is the biggest LGBTQ organization striving for civil rights in America today.

Out & Equal Workplace Advocates
155 Sansome Street, Suite 450
San Francisco, CA 94104
Tel: 415-694-6500
Email: info@outandequal.org
Website: www.outandequal.org

A nonprofit organization that focuses on LGBTQ people in the workplace. They also offer diversity training resources and host an annual Workplace Summit that educates professionals on LGBTQ issues.

List of Web Resources

Alligaytor.com
www.alligaytor.com

Gay Financial Network
http://www.gayalliance.org/directory/gay-financial-network.html

Human Rights Campaign
www.hrc.org/issues/workplace

Gay-Straight Alliance Network
www.gsanetwork.org

National Gay & Lesbian Chamber of Commerce
www.nglcc.org

Progayjobs.com
www.progayjobs.com

Out & Equal Workplace Advocates
www.outandequal.org

OUT for Work
www.outforwork.org

Out Professionals
www.outprofessionals.org

The Williams Institute
www.williamsinstitute.law.ucla.edu

Transworkplace
www.transworkplace.ning.co

References

Chapter 1

Gloria Anzaldua Quote. Equality Forum, http://www.lgbthistorymonth.com/gloria-anzaldua

Madell, Robin, *LGBT: Progress and Problems in the Workplace, Part 1*, The Glasshammer, http://www.theglasshammer. com/news/2012/06/25/lgbt-progress-and-problems-in-the-workplace-part-1/

Lesbian, Gay, Bisexual & Transgender Workplace Issues, Catalyst, http://www.catalyst.org/publication/203/lesbian-gay-bisexual-transgender-workplace-issues

Ernst and Young, *Leading Through Inclusion*, http://www. gcpartnership.com/Economic-Inclusion/Commission/~/media/Files/Inclusion/LGBT%20Leading%20Through%20Inclusion.ashx

Burns Crosby, Krehely, Jeff, *Gay and Transgender People Face High Rates of Workplace Discrimination and Harassment*, http://www.americanprogress.org/issues/lgbt/news/2011/06/02/9872/gay-and-transgender-people-face-high-rates-of-workplace-discrimination-and-harassment/

LGBT Basic Rights and Liberties, ACLU, http://www.aclu. org/lgbt-rights/lgbt-basic-rights-and-liberties

Employment Non-Discrimination Act, Human Rights Campaign, http://www.hrc.org/laws-and-legislation/ federal-legislation/employment-non-discrimination-act

Sexual Orientation Discrimination: Your Rights, Nolo, http:// www.nolo.com/legal-encyclopedia/sexual-orientation-discrimination-rights-29541.html

Santillano, Vicki, *Proud All Year: The Most Gay-Friendly US Cities,* http://www.divinecaroline.com/33/115106-proud-year-most-gay-friendly-u-s#0

Corporate Equality Index 2013. *Rating American Workplaces on Lesbian, Gay, Bisexual and Transgender Equality.* http://www.hrc.org/files/assets/resources/ CorporateEqualityIndex_2013.pdf

Chapter 2

Ramon Cortines Quote. Equality Forum, http://www.lgbthistorymonth.com/ramon-cortines

My Queer Career 2012, slide 1-15
Mulenberg College Staff Development, slide 1-30

Impact of Sexual Orientation on Career Management Skills and Career Progression, http://www.skillsdevelopmentscotland. co.uk/our-story/equality-and-diversity/impact-of-sexual-orientation-on-careers.aspx

Schreier, Kathleen, *Assessing The Career Development and Needs of Lesbian College Students,* The College of Brockport: State University of New York, http://digitalcommons. brockport.edu/cgi/viewcontent.cgi?article=1095&context

Assess Interests, Values, Skills, Work Preferences, Project 10, www.project10.info/DetailPage.php?...Career%20 Development..

Values Assessment, Rutgers, http://careerservices.rutgers. edu/OCAvaluesassessment.shtml

Role Models and Career Development, slide 1-13

Self-Assessment Resources, The Riley Guide, http://www. rileyguide.com/assess.html

Cass Model of Gay/Lesbian Identity Development, Ferris State University, http://www.ferris.edu/HTMLS/studentlife/ PersonalCounseling/students/identity.htm

Chapter 3

Zhou Dan Quote. Equality Forum, http://www.lgbthistorymonth.com/zhou-dan

Creating an LGBT-Friendly Workplace, Lambda Legal, http:// data.lambdalegal.org/pdf/300.pdf

Hill, Peter, *LGBT Rights Law: A Career Guide,* http://www. law.harvard.edu/current/careers/opia/toolkit/guides/ documents/guide-lgbt.pdf

Fricke, Kirsten, *The Influence of Society on Queer Identity Development and Classification,* http://www.uvm. edu/~vtconn/v31/Fricke.pdf

LGBT Career Resource Guide, University of California, http://www.lgbtrc.uci.edu/resourcescareerguide.php

Job Search Advice For LGBT Job Seekers, http://www. glassdoor.com/blog/lgbt-job-seekers/

LGBT Career Development Resources, Duke University Student Affairs, http://studentaffairs.duke.edu/career/ online-tools-resources/lgbt-resources/lgbt-career- development-resources

Chapter 4

Don Lemon Quote. Equality Forum, http://www.lgbthistorymonth.com/don-lemon

Brandis, Jonathan, Brainyquote, http://www.brainyquote. com/quotes/authors/j/jonathan_brandis.html

Role Models and Career Development, slide 1-13

Selig, John R, *Role Models For Gay Youth in America Can Be a Matter of Life and Death,* HWF Magazine, http://www. johnselig.com/commentary/gayyouth/

Cordes, Drew, *The Importance of LGBT Role Models,* http:// www.bilerico.com/2012/11/the_importance_of_lgbt_role_ models.php

On The Important of LBGT Role Models, http://www. thedailypage.com/isthmus/article.php?article=37979

Cherry, Kendra, *Social Learning Theory,* http:// psychology.about.com/od/developmentalpsychology/a/ sociallearning.htm

Social Learning Theory (Bandura), http://www.learning-theories.com/social-learning-theory-bandura.html

Kapp, Karl, *Bandura's Social Learning Theory,* http://www. uleduneering.com/kappnotes/index.php/2011/05/ banduras-social-learning-theory/

Why Do We Need Role Models? Scienceblogs, http:// scienceblogs.com/thusspakezuska/2006/09/27/why-do-we-need-role-models/

Aligning Yourself With The Right Mentor, http://www. chalenejohnson.com/uncategorized/aligning-yourself-with-the-right-mentor/

Chapter 5

Leonardo Da Vinci Quote. Equality Forum,
http://www.lgbthistorymonth.com/leonardo-da-vinci

Leadership, Business Solutions, http://teamaltman.com/
leadership/

Most Inclusive LGBT Employer Named, HC Online, http://
www.hcamag.com/article/most-inclusive-lgbt-employer-
named-129107.aspx

Do You Work For a Fully Inclusive Employer in Memphis?
http://grand-divisions.blogspot.com/2012/10/do-you-
work-for-fully-lgbt-inclusive.html

The Business Case For Pride in Diversity, http://www.
prideindiversity.com.au/why-lgbt-inclusion/

Thompson, Ian, *Working Towards an LGBT-Inclusive Platform*,
http://www.aclu.org/blog/lgbt-rights-religion-belief-
womens-rights/working-towards-lgbt-inclusive-platform

Search Our Employer Database, Resources, Human Rights
Campaign, http://www.aclu.org/blog/lgbt-rights-religion-
belief-womens-rights/working-towards-lgbt-inclusive-
platform

Pearlman, Alex, *5 Leading LGBT Friendly Companies*, http://
www.globalpost.com/dispatches/globalpost-blogs/
rights/5-leading-lgbt-friendly-companies

Hotlist, Out For Work, http://www.outforwork.org/
resources/hotlist.asp

Corporate Equality Index, Human Rights Campaign, http://
www.hrc.org/resources/entry/2012-Corporate-Equality-
Index-Criteria

Corporate Equality Index: 2012 Statements From Employers That Rated 100 Percent, Human Rights Campaign, http://www.hrc.org/resources/entry/corporate-equality-index-2012-statements-from-employers-that-rated-100-perc

The Diversity Inc Top 50 Companies For Diversity, http://www.diversityinc.com/the-diversityinc-top-50-companies-for-diversity-2012/

Chapter 6

Kye Allums Quote. Equality Forum, http://www.lgbthistorymonth.com/kye-allums

Dozetos, Barbara, *Should You Come Out on Your Resume,* http://career-advice.monster.com/resumes-cover-letters/resume-writing-tips/should-you-come-out-on-your-resume/article.aspx

Fowler, Janet, *How Lying On Your Resume With Get You In Trouble,* http://www.myfoxdetroit.com/story/19583396/how-lying-on-your-resume-will-get-you-in-trouble

Larsen, Marie, *How To Write a Great Resume,* http://www.recruiter.com/i/how-to-write-a-great-resume/

Scocco, Daniel, *44 Resume Writing Tips,* Daily Writing Tips, http://www.dailywritingtips.com/resume-writing-tips/

Chapter 7

Tammy Baldwin Quote. Equality Forum, http://www.lgbthistorymonth.com/tammy-baldwin

Job Search Advice For LGBT job Seekers, http://outandequal.wordpress.com/2012/07/12/job-search-advice-for-lgbt-job-seekers/

Interview Success Plan, http://www.job-interview.net/guide/spstep4.htm

Why Gay Men Don't Get Job Interviews, The Week, http://theweek.com/article/index/220029/why-gay-men-dont-get-job-interviews

Simpson, Kareen, *Shout It Out: Gay Man's Guide To a job Interview,* http://voices.yahoo.com/shout-out-gay-mans-guide-job-interview-2303663.html?cat=60

Job Search Advice For LGBT Job Seekers, http://www.glassdoor.com/blog/lgbt-job-seekers/

Chapter 8

Jane Lynch Quote. Equality Forum, http://www.lgbthistorymonth.com/jane-lynch

Williams, Steve, *Report: It's Still Risky To Come Out At Work,* http://www.care2.com/causes/report-its-still-risky-to-come-out-at-work.html

Coming Out, http://www.wetfeet.com/advice-tools/on-the-job/coming-out

Coming Out at Work – One Employees Experiences, http://careers.guardian.co.uk/careers-blog/coming-out-work-employee-experiences

Cahalane, Claudia, *Coming Out at Work: How Easy is it?* http://www.guardian.co.uk/money/2010/nov/13/coming-out-at-work-gay

McKay Dawn, *Coming Out at Work,* http://careerplanning.about.com/od/personalissues/a/coming_out.htm

Coming Out, http://www.gaymanners.com/queeries/how-do-i-come-out-at-work-and-keep-my-job

Belge, Kathy, *Coming Out at Work: Things To Consider Before Coming Out at Work*, http://lesbianlife.about.com/od/comingout/a/OutatWork.htm

Dailey, Kate, *Out at The Office: Loud and Proud*, http://www.bbc.co.uk/news/magazine-18680489

Cipollone, Vince, *Sexuality: Why Honesty is The Best Policy*, http://careers.guardian.co.uk/sexuality-workplace-honesty-lgbt

Chapter 9

John Berry Quote. Equality Forum, http://www.lgbthistorymonth.com/john-berry

Workplace Discrimination, http://civilliberty.about.com/od/gendersexuality/ig/Lesbian-and-Gay-Rights-101/Anti-Gay-Discrimination.htm

LGBT Basic Rights and Liberties, http://www.aclu.org/lgbt-rights/lgbt-basic-rights-and-liberties

Sexual Orientation Discrimination Your Rights, http://www.nolo.com/legal-encyclopedia/sexual-orientation-discrimination-rights-29541.html

Herszenhorn, David, *House Approves Bill Outlawing Workplace Discrimination Against Gays*, http://www.nytimes.com/2007/11/08/world/americas/08iht-congress.4.8252596.html

Anderson, Arnold, *How Do I Prevent Discrimination in The Workplace*, http://smallbusiness.chron.com/prevent-discrimination-workplace-2853.html

How To Avoid Workplace Discrimination, http://wiki.legalexaminer.com/help-center/articles/how-to-avoid-workplace-discrimination.aspx

Legal Resources, http://www.acc.com/legalresources/quickcounsel/pdahitw.cfm

Sexual Orientation Discrimination,

http://www.rightsatwork.co.uk/employment-law/sexual-orientation-discrimination.html

Discrimination and Sexual Orientation, http://www.discriminationonline.com/discrimination/sexual_discrimination.asp

Homosexual Discrimination, http://www.lawlink.nsw.gov.au/lawlink/adb/ll_adb.nsf/pages/adb_homosexual

Gays and Lesbians Face Persistent Workplace Discrimination and Hostility Despite Improved Policies and Attitudes, http://outandequal.org/node/141

Tungol, JR, *Don't Ask Don't Tell One year Repeal Anniversary: 25 Amazing Moments*, http://www.huffingtonpost.com/2012/09/20/dont-ask-dont-tell-repeal-anniversary_n_1891519.html#slide=1515763

Chapter 10

Carolyn Bertozzi Quote. Equality Forum, http://www.lgbthistorymonth.com/carolyn-bertozzi

Smith, Jacquelyn, *Make Social media Your Job Finding Weapon*, http://www.forbes.com/sites/jacquelynsmith/2012/04/20/make-social-media-your-job-finding-weapon/

Bauer, Chad, *10 Ways To Use Social Media To Get a Job*, http://newgradlife.blogspot.com/2009/10/graduate-jobs-business-jobs-careers.html

Nicky, *How Many People Found Jobs Via Social Media?*

Infographic, http://thenickyblog.com/2011/08/people-jobs-social-media-infographic.html

20 Social Networking Sites For Business Professionals, http://wpwidgets.net/20-social-networking-sites-for-business-professionals/

The Many Uses of Social Media: Job opportunity For America's First Gay Travel Guru, http://www.theideabrand.com/2010/04/29/the-many-uses-of-social-media-job-opportunity-for-americas-first-gay-travel-guru/

How To Use Google To Search, http://searchengineland.com/guide/how-to-use-google-to-search

Operators and More Search Help, Google, http://support.google.com/websearch/bin/answer.py?hl=en&answer=136861&rd=1

Chapter 11

Andy Warhol Quote. Equality Forum, http://www.lgbthistorymonth.com/andy-warhol

LGBT Career Development Resources, Duke University, http://studentaffairs.duke.edu/career/online-tools-resources/lgbt-resources/lgbt-career-development-resources

Out Professionals The Nation's Leading Gay and Lesbian Networking Organization, http://www.outprofessionals.org/

Welcome To The Gay Recruiter Network, http://gayrecruiternetwork.com/

Careerproud, *Connecting LGBT Talent With Progressive Employers*, http://www.careerproud.com/
Job Networking Tips, http://www.helpguide.org/life/job_networking_how_to_find_job.htm

Hansen, Randall, *Networking Your Way To a New Job,* http://www.quintcareers.com/networking_guide.html

Resource Guide, Lambda Legal, http://data.lambdalegal.org/publications/downloads/out-at-work_resource.pdf

Conclusion

Georgina Beyer Quote. Equality Forum, http://www.lgbthistorymonth.com/georgina-beyer

About the Author

With a decade of experience in working with lesbian, gay, bisexual, and transgender students, Riley B. Folds founded OUT for Work, the only national nonprofit organization dedicated to educating, preparing and empowering LGBTQ college students and their allies for the transition from academia to the workplace.

In addition, Folds presents across the country to career center professionals and students on the subject of career development for LGBTQ individuals. He is often called upon to present at national conferences such as NACE, ACPA, NASPA, Out & Equal, and MBLGTACC. Further he has often asked to respond to media request on the subject of LGBTQ workplace inclusion.

Folds is also the recipient of the 2013 Public Service Award. Awarded by the American College Personnel Association's Standing Committee for LGBT Awareness, this award recognizes significant contributions to higher education through support and efforts in LGBT awareness.

Folds received his undergraduate degree from La Roche College, Certification in Workplace Diversity Management from Cornell's School of Industrial Relations, and a Master's Degree in Career Counseling from Capella University (2013). He has held senior level positions within the public, private, government, and nonprofit sectors.

In his spare time Folds enjoys working out, watching TV, and spending times with his friends and dogs.

Made in the USA
San Bernardino, CA
20 December 2013